NEW DIRECTIONS FOR ADULT AND CONTINUING EDUCATION

Providing Culturally Relevant Adult Education: A Challenge for the Twenty-First Century

Talmadge C. Guy
University of Georgia

EDITOR

Number 82, Summer 1999

JOSSEY-BASS PUBLISHERS
San Francisco

PROVIDING CULTURALLY RELEVANT ADULT EDUCATION: A CHALLENGE FOR THE TWENTY-FIRST CENTURY
Talmadge C. Guy (ed.)
New Directions for Adult and Continuing Education, no. 82
Susan Imel, Editor-in-Chief

Microfilm copies of issues and articles are available in 16mm and 35mm, as well as microfiche in 105mm, through University Microfilms Inc., 300 North Zeeb Road, Ann Arbor, Michigan 48106-1346.

ISSN 1052-2891 ISBN 0-7879-1167-4

NEW DIRECTIONS FOR ADULT AND CONTINUING EDUCATION is part of The Jossey-Bass Higher and Adult Education Series and is published quarterly by Jossey-Bass Inc., Publishers, 350 Sansome Street, San Francisco, California 94104-1342. Periodicals postage paid at San Francisco, California, and at additional mailing offices. Postmaster: Send address changes to New Directions for Adult and Continuing Education, Jossey-Bass Inc., Publishers, 350 Sansome Street, San Francisco, California 94104-1342.

SUBSCRIPTIONS cost $58.00 for individuals and $104.00 for institutions, agencies, and libraries.

EDITORIAL CORRESPONDENCE should be sent to the Editor-in-Chief, Susan Imel, ERIC/ACVE, 1900 Kenny Road, Columbus, Ohio 43210-1090. E-mail: imel.1@osu.edu.

Cover photograph by Wernher Krutein/PHOTOVAULT © 1990.

Jossey-Bass Web address: http://www.josseybass.com

Contents

EDITOR'S NOTES

The field of adult education has moved slowly toward theorizing within particular social and cultural contexts as opposed to viewing adult education knowledge as applicable to all learners, despite the context. Previous sourcebooks (for example, Hayes and Colin, 1994; Ross-Gordon, Martin, and Briscoe, 1990) have focused on the identification of shortcomings within the adult education literature concerning issues of race, gender, and class. This volume continues in that vein but offers an examination of theoretical and practical issues in providing adult education services to socially, politically, and culturally marginalized groups in the United States. Particular emphasis is given to learner culture; contributors to the volume share the cultural background of the teachers and learners in the programs they discuss.

This volume is premised on the basic but important assumption that culture is central to shaping and molding the adult education process. Furthermore, an analysis of culturally based adult education provides a means of access to empower oppressed people to gain greater control over their lives. This volume sets out to examine the ways in which that is true. The principal strategy is to focus on marginalized groups in American society and thereby to illustrate the ways in which culture shapes adult education. Beyond this, the contributors identify ways in which educators and trainers of adults can help marginalized and disadvantaged learners take control of their circumstances through adult education.

The importance of identifying authors who possess "insider knowledge" (Hill-Collins, 1990) of the culture being represented cannot be overestimated. I invited authors with significant research knowledge as well as practical experience in serving the cultural groups they write about. The number of authors with both research and practical experience is limited with respect to culturally marginalized groups in the United States. Unfortunately, activists typically do not associate with researchers and vice versa. Hence, for some groups, such as Asian Americans and Native Americans, I had great difficulty in merely identifying potential authors. Fortunately, I found a contributor for a chapter on Native American adult education but was not able to find one for a chapter on Asian American adult education. Many stories are yet to be told and, with time, I am confidant they will be told. Let this be a first step in that direction.

Second, it was important to reflect adult education in various domains of practice, policy, teaching, curriculum, and program planning. In inviting the authors to contribute, I requested that a variety of adult education domains be addressed, including those mentioned, and many did so.

The chapters presented here, then, address the issue of culture as it is employed in various sociocultural contexts and in relation to specific educational and social problems. In Chapter One, I show how the definition of the word *culture* is significant for adult educators working with marginalized populations of adults. I then discuss what it means for adult education to be culturally relevant.

In Chapter Two, Donna D. Amstutz discusses adult learning theory. She identifies ways that traditional theory has been inadequate to account for the many cultural differences manifested in adult education programs and in ethnic-racial-cultural communities. She suggests theoretical and practical alternatives for adult educators working in culturally marginalized communities.

In Chapter Three, Vanessa Sheared develops her Africentric feminist model of adult education for African American adult literacy learners. She offers suggestions for adult educators to improve the retention of African American learners in the adult basic education classroom. Important factors in this process include communicative, social, and cultural issues that can be used in crafting instruction for adult learners. But she warns about the impact of limited resources in programs serving African American learners and suggests that adult educators be cognizant of the political and social impact of their work.

In Chapter Four, Jorge Jeria discusses a variety of issues related to serving Hispanics in adult education. He reviews the politics involved in identifying all Spanish-speaking adults as Hispanics. He offers a critique of adult education based on human capital theory and suggests popular education as a model for adult educators to draw on in developing programs for Hispanics.

In Chapter Five, Louise Lockard describes the experience of Navajo Indian adult education with its focus on traditional Navajo language. She argues that culture is central to reclaiming Navajo identity and community as a means to lifting Navajo adults out of the poverty and despair that afflicts many Native Americans.

In Chapter Six, Elizabeth A. Peterson addresses policy issues relative to culturally relevant adult education for African Americans. She traces the historical development of theories of African American adult education and relates these to contemporary analyses of race based on critical race theory. She lists a number of recommendations for adult educators to improve services for African American adults.

In Chapter Seven, I identify common themes raised by the contributors to this volume and conclude with a brief discussion of issues that adult education practitioners should consider in implementing culturally relevant programs.

Why is this effort important? At bottom, the answer is straightforward. Adult learners will be very different in the future, and the sociocultural background of learners will become increasingly important in shaping how adult education services are provided for racially, ethnically, and linguistically marginalized learners. I hope this issue of *New Directions for Adult and*

Continuing Education will serve as an important point of reference for adult educators who serve these populations and for adult education scholars who are rethinking their approach to adult education for the twenty-first century.

Talmadge C. Guy
Editor

References

Hayes, E., and Colin, S. *Confronting Racism and Sexism in Adult Education.* New Directions for Adult and Continuing Education, no. 61. San Francisco: Jossey-Bass, 1994.

Ross-Gordon, J., Martin, L., and Briscoe, D. *Serving Culturally Diverse Populations.* New Directions for Adult and Continuing Education, no. 48. San Francisco: Jossey-Bass, 1990.

TALMADGE C. GUY is assistant professor in the Department of Adult Education at the University of Georgia, Athens.

1

Culturally relevant adult education can help learners validate their cultural identity and use their cultural knowledge as a basis for personal and social transformation.

Culture as Context for Adult Education: The Need for Culturally Relevant Adult Education

Talmadge C. Guy

The United States has been, is, and will continue to be a culturally diverse society. Despite this diversity of culture, however, the nation continues to be dominated by a macroculture (Naylor, 1998) that emphasizes Anglo-Western-European cultural values. Education has been a primary means of socializing individuals into mainstream culture. By the time children grow into adulthood, they have learned who matters, what priorities are important, and with whom and how to interact. Every aspect of adult life is shaped by culture, and education has served as a vehicle for defining the cultural values that people hold or that they view as central to being successful in their society.

When people learn about who matters and what's important in their lives, they can either be empowered or marginalized, depending on their own personal and cultural history. All too often, it is persons whose group identity is socially, politically, and economically marginalized—for example, African Americans, Native Americans, Hispanic Americans, and Asian Americans—who are most affected by the cultural mismatch between the learning environment and their own cultural history. This chapter argues that culturally relevant adult education is essential to helping learners from marginalized cultural backgrounds learn to take control of their lives and improve their social condition (Hollins, King, and Hayman, 1994).

What does it mean for adult education to be culturally relevant? What is different or important about educating adults in a culturally relevant way? The answers to these questions lie in an understanding of the importance of the role that culture plays in shaping the educational process. Therefore, it will be necessary to examine the concept of culture, especially the role that cultural domination plays in privileging some and subordinating others.

Why should adult educators be concerned about these issues? Certain moral and political arguments suggest that helping the marginalized is the good or prudent thing to do. Whether or not adult educators are individually predisposed to focusing on the problems and issues of the marginalized, inevitable demographic trends are prompting many to reexamine their assumptions and values with regard to the adult education process. For example, adult educators are accustomed to data indicating that adult education programs typically serve the middle-class, employed, and usually white adult learner (Merriam and Brockett, 1997; Ross-Gordon, 1990). With the possible exception of the area of adult basic education (ABE) programs, which typically serve a higher proportion of adults from minority, poor, and undereducated groups, much adult education theory and practice is based on the white, middle-class experience (Flannery, 1994). Although the majority of learners in ABE classes are white, significantly more African Americans, Hispanic Americans, and other ethnic, linguistic, or racial minority groups are in that area than are in other areas of adult education (Martin, 1990). As the numbers of racially, ethnically, and linguistically marginalized learners increase, new approaches to teaching and learning based on the sociocultural experiences and backgrounds of the population must be developed.

Perspectives on Culture

Noted British cultural critic and activist, Raymond Williams, observes that *culture* is one of the two or three most complicated words in the English language (Williams, 1983). Kroeber and Kluckhohn (1952) list 164 definitions of *culture*, as the term is used in the social sciences. In addition, everyday usage includes *high culture, popular culture, organizational culture, ethnic culture, subculture*, and *uncultured*—only a few of the dizzying assortment of uses.

The etymology of the word *culture* reveals its multiple meanings. Derived from the Latin word *cultura*, the English word originally referred to activities related to agriculture—cultivating or tending. By the nineteenth century, culture had also come to refer to the manners and social graces associated with the elite and the educated. Nineteenth-century British cultural critic, Matthew Arnold (1994), popularized this new concept of culture, defining it as "contact with the best which has been thought and said in the world." Arnold saw culture as crucial to a democratic society because of culture's important qualities such as beauty, intelligence, and perfection. Arnold believed that by striving to achieve these qualities in its citizens, democracy would prosper because individuals who acquire culture are enlightened and possess an excellence of taste acquired by formal educational and moral training. For Arnold, these qualities of culture were universal and the same for all human societies. Moreover, Arnold's perspective held that culture is acquired over time through rigorous training as defined by the elite.

Arnold's conception of culture was the prevailing definition in the United States until perhaps the mid-twentieth century. Adult educators like Horace Kallen (1924) and Alain Locke (1944) proposed broader and more inclusive definitions of culture. For both Kallen and Locke, culture was an attribute of the "folk," the people—not simply of the educated or the elite. Kallen (1915) coined the term *cultural pluralism* to refer to a society in which different cultural groups would coexist democratically and peacefully. Influenced partly by the reformist nature of pragmatic philosophy but also motivated by the ethnic and racial politics of the day, Kallen believed that public life within the larger society would be all the richer because of the unique contributions of the variety of ethnic cultures. Locke wrote about the experiences of African Americans in adult education. For Locke, culture is baked into the "daily bread" of a people's life (Locke, 1989). Culture is what defines who they are—how they view themselves and the world around them.

However, it was not until the 1960s that the Arnoldian conception of culture began to be replaced with another definition. Based on the work of anthropologists, a new definition emerged that defined culture as the totality of socially transmitted behavior patterns, arts, beliefs, institutions, and all other products of creativity. Relatedly, culture has come be understood as "the integrated pattern of human knowledge, belief, and behavior that depends upon man's capacity for learning and transmitting knowledge to succeeding generations (Herskovits, 1955, p. 4).

The popular definition of culture has come to refer to the shared values, attitudes, beliefs, behaviors, and language use within a social group. These cultural values and beliefs and practices are at the core of group life and identity and are powerful factors that shape or influence individual attitudes, beliefs, and behaviors. In other words, culture is omnipresent and is essential to human social life.

Controlling Culture. Despite the theoretical movement toward a more democratic or popular conception of culture, the Arnoldian version of high culture remains influential. It is fashionable nowadays for political and educational leaders to bemoan the decline in culture that they say is characteristic of contemporary American society. From E. D. Hirsch's *Cultural Literacy: What Every American Needs to Know* (1987) and Allan Bloom's *The Closing of the American Mind* (1987) to conservative politicians like Pat Buchanan and Dan Quayle, the criticism of a popular culture gone berserk at the expense of traditional cultural values is the sounding alarm for a political and religious backlash against non-Anglo, non-Western cultural perspectives. The control for the production and validation of culture remains an important issue that drives much public discussion and debate about the future of American society.

It is one thing to consider that culture is central to understanding human activity. It is quite another to consider the ways in which elites attempt to control cultural processes and means of production, which raises the question, Who has the power and authority over the processes by which culture is produced? For example, most dominant world cultures have been patriarchal. Western European culture has been the most dominant and transcendent of all world cultures in the past five hundred years (West, 1993). Historically, dominant cultures have systematically limited the power of women and people of color in their social, political, and religious institutions. Although important changes have taken place to advance women's and African Americans' civil rights since World War II, it is still an indication of the change that yet needs to occur that women and African Americans, among others, continue to be underrepresented politically and undercompensated economically for equal work. These structural realities of American society are indicative of the underlying cultural differences that pit Eurocentric cultural traditions against Africentric, Hispanic, Native American and other ethnic cultural traditions.

To question who has the power to determine culture serves as a reminder of the imbalance in the distribution of power between those who identify with mainstream cultural traditions and those who, in the spirit of democratic and popular culture, seek to redefine their identities and social practices in terms of marginalized cultural perspectives. In this discussion of the definition of culture, we should not only ask how culture is defined but who has the power and authority to enforce a particular definition. Therefore, we must examine any answer to the question, What is culture?, and ask what the implications of that answer are for the poor, the marginalized, and the less powerful in our society. To the extent that the answer excludes these people, the possibility of meaningful change in the lives of learners from marginalized cultures is diminished. Change cannot be achieved because these learners continue to operate within the cultural norms, values, and traditions of a dominant culture.

Cultural Diversity and Changing Demographics. The analysis of definitions of culture is more than a merely intellectual exercise. The practical demographic realities facing the United States make it an essential activity for adult educators. Even though the United States has always been a culturally diverse society, the *significance* of that diversity has rarely been as important as it is today. Demographic trends indicate that the population is changing from one that is predominantly white and of European ancestry to one that is more heterogeneous, with significant proportions of African Americans, Hispanic Americans, and Asian Americans. Although Native Americans will represent a substantially smaller proportion of the population than these groups, their numbers are projected to rise somewhat.

More than nine million immigrants entered the United States from Asian and Latin American nations in the twenty-year period from 1970 to 1990. As a result the Hispanic American population almost tripled from 1970 to 1990, reaching close to thirty million. Similarly, the Asian American population has increased ninefold as compared with pre-1970 levels and now exceeds nine million (U.S. Bureau of the Census, 1996). The African American population continues to grow at a faster rate than the European American population and will exceed thirty-three million by the year 2000. These changes have meant a shift in the composition of the U.S. population such that persons of color now represent one in four citizens (Hing, 1997; Lassiter, 1998). And current projections suggest that the relative proportion of whites to nonwhites could reach 50–50 by the year 2050 (Hing, 1997). These changes in the composition of the U.S. population mean that accepted Eurocentric cultural traditions and practices will increasingly be subject to question and challenge. The process has already begun.

One cautionary note is required here, however. As is always the case when discussing group-level characteristics and issues, one runs the risk of oversimplification or of overgeneralization. It is therefore advisable to qualify any discussion about the status of ethnic or cultural groups by saying that individuals within groups may have different experiences from those described as characteristic of the group. And so the discussion that follows proceeds with an acknowledgment that individuals are not determined by their group affiliations or identification. But this acknowledgment need not minimize the practical significance of the points made because many, if not most, persons within the groups described do experience some aspect of the group-level descriptions.

Assimilation Versus Separation. From early in U.S. history, European Americans have constituted the vast majority of citizens. Although strong ethnic affiliations and communities persist within this population, the large majority of whites see themselves as American, not as ethnic Americans or "hyphenated Americans," for example, as Italian-American, German-American, Anglo-American, and so on. Whereas European ethnic groups often entered the mainstream by becoming Americanized (Carlson, 1987), persons of color and of non-European ancestry remained separate. Even when European Americans retained a sense of ethnicity, it was not in the same way that excluded minorities did. Michael Novak's (1996) description of the "new ethnicity" among European Americans from Eastern and Southern Europe suggests that, although many European Americans acknowledge their ethnic lineage, they are uneasy about identifying themselves as ethnic American, preferring instead to see themselves only as American. He writes, "Many Southern and Eastern European-Americans have been taught, as I was, not to be "ethnic," or even "hyphenated," but only "American" (p. 347).

Ethnic identity among many European Americans is weakened by a more basic desire to self-identify as part of the larger human community. Ironically, then, American individualism and ethnic identity go hand in hand in the sense that one can have a loose sense of affiliation with an ethnic past while seeing oneself as an individual not bound by the language, traditions, or customs of traditional ethnic culture. Novak notes: "Being 'universal' is regarded as being good; being ethnically self-conscious raises anxieties." Because one's whole identity has been based on being universal, one is "often loath to change public face too suddenly" (p. 346).

Mainstream American Culture and European American Ethnic Identity. In light of the earlier discussion, it should not be too surprising that many European Americans, and even persons of non-European descent, especially those who have achieved some level of educational or occupational success, view discussions about cultural difference with caution and suspicion. The emphasis on cultural differences suggests a tearing apart of American society—a destructive kind of particularism (Ravitch, 1991) that emphasizes racial and ethnic chauvinism over a general sense of American community. The criticism of race- or ethnic-based educational programs is often based on the belief that they are divisive and neither effective nor necessary. Samuel Betances (1985), writing about bilingual education, describes the position of the critics of ethnic culture who say, "My folks made it without bilingual education, what's wrong with yours?" (p. 7).

The tendency of white, middle-class Americans to question the experience of people of color from the perspective of their own ethnic experience suggests a broad view within U.S. mainstream culture that strives to diminish the significance of cultural differences within the population. One of the most active voices representing this view is an Asian Indian, Dinesh D'Souza, who argues that African Americans should follow the example of ethnic Europeans who immigrated and assimilated into mainstream American society (D'Souza, 1995). However, this view overlooks or minimizes the painful and distinct history and experience of people of color. The fact that European immigrants encountered different social and historical conditions than Chinese, Mexicans, Native Americans, or African Americans is largely understandable from the perspective of white privilege (McIntosh, 1990; Scheurich, 1993).

Culture, Difference, and Power. Although it may be said that cultural differences are ever endemic to American society, all cultures are not equally regarded. Carlson (1996) observes that, from its beginnings the United States has always privileged a monocultural standard favoring Anglo and Western European cultural traditions. Although the melting pot metaphor has characterized the way Americans have traditionally responded to the needs of minority groups, the historical actuality for many groups has negated the veracity of the metaphor. African Americans, Hispanic Americans, Native Americans, and Asian Americans continue to experience discrimination. But just as important, the culture of these minority groups is viewed negatively.

Furthermore, the assimilationist model advocated by D'Souza, for example, simply does not reflect the experience of African Americans and other groups. Ogbu refers to these groups as caste-like, indicating the resistance that mainstream white Americans feel toward accepting people of color into American society. The fact of the matter is that the assimilation model simply is not a viable option for some social groups (Novak, 1996).

The Dominant Culture. The idea of dominant culture is not far removed from the idea of mainstream culture. "Dominant culture" adds the component of power to "mainstream culture" and points to issues of oppression, discrimination, and exclusion. Dominant cultural standards are emphasized and are easily identifiable to anyone familiar with American society. Naylor (1998) says, "If one accepts the notion that culture exists in ideas that then generate behavior, they [sic] have to conclude that American culture does exist in this suggestion of a mainstream culture in America, that body of ideas usually associated with the middle class" (p. 47). He goes on to identify a set of ideas that form the core of American mainstream culture such as individualism, freedom, toleration and nonconformity, materialism, and Christianity.

It is a mistake to assume that U.S. mainstream culture is characteristic of all groups in U.S. society. Those groups that do not conform to mainstream culture or who are viewed as being outside the mainstream assume a marginalized status and are oppressed. Minority status is highly associated with prejudice and discrimination. Although in common parlance, *minority* is usually taken to mean minority in numbers, the term more properly refers to low social status and lack of power within a highly stratified American society. Low status and asymmetrical power relations are associated with institutional arrangements that go beyond individual prejudice discrimination to reinforce the subordinate position of minorities.

In turn, negative beliefs and stereotypes are learned through mainstream cultural institutions and practices. Children receive systematic training from parents and from institutionalized sources such as the media about their roles in society and those of other groups. Absent any contravening influences, both white and African American adults "know" that *white* means right, good, normal and that *black* means less, bad, abnormal. Internalizing this permits white adults to be able to say, for example, "I am not prejudiced—but I don't want to live in a predominantly black neighborhood, and I do not want my children to attend a majority black school." These lessons produce stereotypes and myths and influence individual thought and behavior. This cycle of socialization (Harro, cited in Adams, Brigham, Delpes, and Marchesani, 1996) suggests how oppression is reproduced through culturally defined processes of learning. Thus stereotypes, myths, prejudice, and discrimination are reinforced and persist throughout society.

Consequences of Oppression. Both majority and minority persons are affected by the reproduction of oppression. Those persons who enjoy material and social privilege based on race, gender, or ethnicity (or other forms of privilege) often suffer from fear of crime and violence at the hands of minority group members. The rise in the number of gated communities that offer a sense of security can be correlated with white, middle-class, culturally derived perceptions of racially, ethnically, or linguistically different people. Minorities often are blamed for the deprivation they experience such as poverty, crime, illiteracy, and drug addiction. Further, conservative ideologues argue that minorities are a drain on public tax dollars for social services. Within this environment, persons who are members of low-status social groups that are relatively powerless often internalize negative and destructive individual and group identities, which results in low expectations for life chances.

Majority group members hold the power to define and manipulate social space in ways that secure their sense of physical comfort and safety. Consequently, in many urban and suburban communities white, middle- and upper-class individuals restrict the number of minorities who are able to gain access to their communities and institutions such as educational, financial, and cultural and recreational establishments and organizations. Thus it is difficult to find large numbers of African Americans who are members of suburban country clubs or metropolitan civic boards. The absence of an appreciable number of persons of color serves to reinforce the myth that there are very few, if any, African Americans who merit participation in such organizations.

Moreover, minorities are then denied access to the kinds of public and private resources that can facilitate political or economic progress. Many predominantly minority communities are poor, undereducated, crime-ridden, and drug-infested, and they lack an institutional infrastructure to adequately deal with the problems facing them. Financial or material resources available at a grassroots level for community development or for group empowerment are minimal. Nevertheless, this cycle of oppression and its psychological and material consequences can be interrupted. Adult education serves as a fundamental resource for breaking this cycle.

Culturally Relevant Adult Education

Because learning is essential to cultural reproduction, learning is also a central way of combating cultural domination and oppression. Focusing on culture as both object and subject of individual and group learning serves as a way of breaking the destructive cycle of racial, gender, and ethnic oppression. This understanding of culture-based adult education has implications for adult educators who work with persons from traditionally marginalized social groups. In the context of culturally relevant education, then, educators have begun to question the relationship between the cultural origins of adult learners and the educational setting in which adults participate (Martin, 1990; Sheared, 1994; Colin, 1994). It is not enough simply to be culturally inclusive in a pluralistic environment (Moe, 1990). Inclusion does not guarantee equity. Rather, educational norms, processes, and goals must be reevaluated for their potential to assist learners whose individual and group identities are most at risk in terms of the dominant culture's definition of success.

The nature of the fit between learners' cultural backgrounds and their educational experiences is of central concern because of culture's importance in establishing criteria for success or failure. Thus, a principal focus of the educational experience, from the perspective of cultural relevance, is the reconstruction of learners' group-based identity from one that is negative to one that is positive. Learners from marginalized cultural backgrounds too often resort to a rejection of dominant cultural norms and standards (Ogbu, 1992; Quigley, 1990). However, such a stance consigns those individuals to further marginalization and exclusion (Darder, 1991). For adult educators interested in addressing the ways in which cultural domination affects learners in adult education settings, educational strategies must be developed to minimize the potential for further exclusion and marginalization of learners.

Biculturalism

Central to asserting a positive cultural identity so as to challenge racist, sexist, ethnocentric perspectives and practices is the learning that helps learners understand their culture and its value. Members of marginalized groups are, by virtue of the discrimination they face, forced to accommodate themselves to the dominant culture or be even further marginalized. One educational response to this situation is termed *biculturalism*. Darder (1991) argues that biculturalism should frame educational environments. She defines biculturalism as "a process wherein individuals learn to function in two distinct sociocultural environments: their primary culture, and that of the dominant mainstream culture of the society in which they live" (p. 48). This view of biculturalism is similar to the "double consciousness" concept of W.E.B. Du Bois (1990), who wrote that African Americans maintain a double consciousness by virtue of being both African and American. This double consciousness cannot be transcended but, Du Bois argued, can be reconciled, given the right social circumstances.

Other observers of color have made similar observations about the dual nature of minority identity in American society. Darder (1996, p. 49) states that "many studies of Black, Latino, Asian and Native American populations clearly indicate that a bicultural phenomenon is present in the development of people of color. They also support the notion of biculturalism as a mechanism of survival that constitutes forms of adaptive alternatives in the face of hegemonic control and institutional oppression."

Biculturalism is based on a philosophy of cultural democracy (Darder, 1996), asserting that people of color who come from subordinate cultures have the right to maintain their home culture as well as to become competent in the mainstream culture. Cultural democracy, then, refers to the goal of living in a society in which a multiplicity of cultures not only coexists but thrives. From this perspective, monocultural norms and practices must be rejected in favor of a restructuring of cultural and social processes that are broadly inclusive. For adult educators this requires an examination of educational practices to make them culturally relevant to the needs and cultural backgrounds of learners.

Redefining the Norm. In his book, *The Interpretation of Cultures* (1973),Clifford Geertz argues that culture is essentially about shared meaning within a group. He identifies the importance of the symbolic—what he calls "systems of meaning" in the study of culture. He writes, "The concept of culture I espouse . . . [is] that man is an animal suspended in webs of significance he himself has spun. I take culture to be those webs, and the analysis of it to be therefore not an experimental science in search of law but an interpretative one in search of meaning" (pp. 4–5).

If we consider human action as essentially symbolic action, whenever we observe behaviors of people who are different from us, we should ask what is the significance or meaning of that action or behavior. Geertz says, "The thing to ask [of actions] is what their import is" (pp. 9–10). Understanding the significance or meaning of an action involves observing, questioning, and examining, and subsequently reformulating our own assumptions about what the action means. This is possible because, as Geertz asserts, cultures are open to interpretation by outsiders, as cultural meaning is a property of groups rather than individuals. Consequently, we should inquire among "insiders" as to what the action means, or we should seek assistance from someone in a position to know.

Applying Geertz's analysis to the adult education classroom, adult educators who observe learner behavior can raise questions about learner actions. By asking, What is the significance or the meaning that learners attach to their actions in the classroom?, adult educators can obtain a clearer understanding of how congruent learner and teacher perspectives are. When there is a significant difference in socialization between teachers and learners, it is vital that teachers question their assumptions about their learners' actions. For example, white, middle-class, female adult educators who have lived in middle-class homes and who work with African American single mothers may believe they have something in common with their students as either women or as mothers. Yet the barrier of race and class can lead to important misinterpretations and misunderstandings about how learners view the learning environment. In other words, the system of meaning shared among the students may be quite different from the beliefs, assumptions, and values of the instructor.

Rethinking Practice. Teaching in a culturally relevant way requires that adult educators examine the learning environment for communicative processes, instructional practices, classroom norms and expectations, learning evaluation criteria, and instructional content that is potentially culturally incompatible with the learners' culture. Marchisani and Adams (1992) present a useful model that can assist instructors in conceptualizing the classroom from a culturally relevant perspective. The model addresses four elements of the learning environment that should be examined through the lens of culture: (1) the instructor's cultural identity, (2) the learners' cultural identity, (3) the curriculum, and (4) instructional methods and processes.

Instructor Cultural Self-Awareness. First, adult educators must engage in a process of self-examination about their own cultural identity. Because all human beings are essentially cultural beings, any examination of the cultural aspect of the learning environment requires that teachers also examine their own cultural beliefs, assumptions, values, attitudes, and behaviors. Individuals who are monocultural are especially vulnerable to misinterpretation of learners' actions and speech if the learners come from different ethnic, racial, or linguistic backgrounds (Adams, 1992). Rather than view learners from an ethnocentric perspective, that is, one's own cultural norms and standards, adult educators should suspend belief in their own cultural values and beliefs in order to find the meaning that learners attach to learning activities, processes, and materials (Colin and Preciphs, 1991). For example, a teacher who has chosen individual study time for learners who are accustomed to interacting in group work and in conversational style will need to reexamine the value and meaning of individualized learning in light of learners' cultural background.

Learner Culture. Adult educators sometimes find themselves responsible for the learning of students with whom they share little in common. Whenever teacher and learner cultural backgrounds differ, teachers should find a way to learn about who their learners are. Using Geertz's concept of "systems of meaning," understanding learner culture means, in a practical sense, discovering how learners attach meaning to every aspect of the educational environment. In describing elements of culturally relevant education, Ladson-Billings (1994) makes the point that while the racial identity, personality, teaching style, or educational philosophy of effective teachers of African American children may differ, these teachers *know* their students and their culture. They spend time in the communities where their students live. They feel culturally comfortable among their students even though they, themselves, may come from an entirely different cultural background. Simply knowing, or perhaps more accurately thinking that one knows, about heroes or about the music of a particular culture group is not sufficient. Educators of adults are well advised to follow Ladson-Billings' recommendation: know your students and their cultural background and use this information effectively and creatively during instruction (Ladson-Billings, 1994).

Inclusive Curricula. Adult educators should examine the curriculum to ensure that it does not contain stereotypical material or material that does not encompass learners' experiences. Colin describes the importance of selfethnic reflectors in the curriculum for African Americans (Colin, 1989). Course content that stereotypes the very learners it is designed to serve does those learners an injustice. Insensitive or unknowing teachers can overlook material that learners may find offensive or simply irrelevant to their daily lives. Sheared (1994; this volume) emphasizes the importance of connecting with learners' lived experiences. To the extent that classroom materials do not relate to learners' life experiences, these materials become irrelevant and ineffective in facilitating learning. Teachers should examine materials to ensure that they do not stereotype and that they do not exclude learners. For example, if a class of Native American learners reads literacy materials that do not relate to their cultural backgrounds and that contain stereotypical images and representations of Native Americans, those materials do those learners an injustice.

Instructional Methods and Processes. Finally, instructional methods and processes that include or exclude learners require careful attention. The adult education literature is replete with examples of how teachers should share power and responsibility for learning (Apps, 1996; Brookfield; 1986, 1995; Knowles, 1980; Johnson-Bailey and Cervero, 1996; Tisdell, 1995). The sharing of power between teachers and students is of vital importance in culturally diverse classrooms. However teachers honor the responsibility to ensure that classroom dynamics allow for maximum participation of all learners, care must also be exercised to avoid requiring just one form of communication. Chinese American learners, for example, may be uneasy volunteering to lead a class discussion because of their cultural values (Pratt, 1996). Issues of power (and who has it), inclusion, and participation are important elements of the culturally relevant adult classroom. Teachers should attend to classroom processes that maximize learner participation and power sharing.

Conclusion

Current trends in demographic changes in the United States will heighten the awareness and tension between mainstream American cultural values and practices and those of marginalized minorities and non-European immigrants. Learners from socially, politically, and economically disenfranchised groups are highly susceptible to being alienated by educational practices based on mainstream cultural values. Effective learning among these learners demands that adult educators reorient educational practices to incorporate learners' culture into the educational process.

Culturally relevant adult education requires more than a simple knowledge of techniques and methods. Cultural self-awareness and detailed cultural knowledge of learners is best achieved through experiential learning. Adult educators should find ways to learn about the cultural backgrounds of their learners and to discover learners' webs of significance. Cultural self-awareness, cultural knowledge about learners, and instructional skills that are inclusive and empowering constitute the kind of knowledge and skills required for service to marginalized learners.

References

Adams, M. (ed.). *Promoting Diversity in College Classrooms: Innovative Responses for the Curriculum, Faculty, and Institutions.* San Francisco: Jossey-Bass, 1992.

Apps, J. W. *Teaching from the Heart.* Malabar, Fla.: Krieger, 1996.

Arnold, M. *Culture and Anarchy.* New Haven, Conn.: Yale University Press, 1994.

Betances, S. "My People Made It Without Bilingual Education, What's Wrong with Your People?" *Official Journal of the California School Boards Association*, 1985, *44* (7).

Bloom, A. *The Closing of the American Mind.* New York: Simon & Schuster, 1987.

Brookfield, S. *Understanding and Facilitating Adult Learning.* San Francisco: Jossey-Bass, 1986.

Brookfield, S. *Becoming a Critically Reflective Teacher.* San Francisco: Jossey-Bass, 1995.

Carlson, R. *The Americanization Syndrome: A Quest for Conformity.* New York: St. Martin's Press, 1987.

Colin, S.A.J., III."Cultural Literacy: Ethnocentrism v. Selfethnic Reflectors." In *Thresholds,* Northern Illinois University, 1989.

Colin, S.A.J., III. "Adults and Continuing Education Graduate Programs: Prescriptions for the Future." In *Racism and Sexism in the United States: Fundamental Issues.* New Directions for Adult and Continuing Education, no. 61. San Francisco: Jossey-Bass, 1994.

Colin, S.A.J., III, and Preciphs, T. "Perceptual Patterns and the Learning Environment: Confronting White Racism." In *Creating an Effective Learning Environment.* New Directions for Adult and Continuing Education, no. 50. San Francisco: Jossey-Bass, 1991.

D'Souza, D. *The End of Racism: Principles for a Multiracial Society.* New York: Free Press, 1995.

Darder, A. *Culture and Power in the Classroom: A Critical Foundation for Bicultural Education.* New York: Bergin & Garvey, 1991.

Darder, A. *Culture and Power in the Classroom.* Westport, CT: Bergin and Garvey, 1996.

Du Bois, W.E.B. *The Souls of Black Folk.* New York: Vintage Books, 1990.

Flannery, D. "Changing Dominant Understandings of Adults as Learners." In E. Hayes and S. Colin (eds.), *Confronting Racism and Sexism in Adult Education.* New Directions for Adult and Continuing Education, no. 61. San Francisco: Jossey-Bass, 1994.

Geertz, C. *The Interpretation of Cultures: Selected Essays.* New York: Basic Books, 1973.

Harro, B. "Cycle of Socialization." In M. Adams, P. Brigha, P. Dalpes, and L. Marchesani (eds.), *Diversity and Oppression: Conceptual Frameworks.* Dubuque, Iowa: Kendall/Hunt, 1996.

Herskovits, M. J. *Cultural Anthropology.* New York: Knopf, 1955.

Hing, B. O. *To Be American.* New York: New York University Press, 1997.

Hirsch, E. D. *Cultural Literacy: What Every American Needs to Know.* Boston: Houghton-Mifflin, 1987.

Hollins, E. R., King, J. E., and Hayman, W. C. *Teaching Diverse Populations: Formulating a Knowledge Base.* Albany, N.Y.: State University of New York Press, 1994.

Johnson-Bailey, J., and Cervero, R. M. "An Analysis of the Educational Narratives of Reentry Black Women." *Adult Education Quarterly,* 1996, *46* (3).

Kallen, H. "Democracy and the Melting Pot: A Study of American Nationality." *The Nation,* 1915, *100,* 190–194; 216–220.

Kallen, H. *Culture and Democracy in the United States: Studies in the Group Psychology of the American Peoples.* New York: Boni and Liverwright, 1924.

Knowles, M. *The Modern Practice of Adult Education: From Pedagogy to Andragogy.* Chicago: Association Press, 1980.

Kroeber, A. L., and Kluckhohn, C. *Culture: A Critical Review of Concepts and Definitions.* Cambridge, Mass.: Peabody Museum of American Archaeology and Ethnology, Harvard University, 1952.

Ladson-Billings, G. *The Dreamkeepers: Successful Teachers of African American Children.* San Francisco: Jossey-Bass, 1994.

Locke, A. "Frontiers of Culture." In *The Philosophy of Alain Locke: Harlem Renaissance and Beyond.* Philadelphia: Temple University Press, 1989.

Marchisani, L., and Adams, M. "The Dynamics of Diversity in the Teaching and Learning Process: A Faculty Development Model for Analysis and Action." In L. Marchisani and M. Adams (eds.), *Promoting Diversity in College Classrooms.* San Francisco: Jossey-Bass, 1992.

Martin, L. M. "Facilitating Cultural Diversity in Adult Literacy Programs." In J. M. Ross-Gordon, L. G. Martin, and B. D. Briscoe, (eds.), *Serving Culturally Diverse Populations.* New Directions for Adult and Continuing Education, no. 49. San Francisco: Jossey-Bass, 1990.

McIntosh, P. "Unpacking the Knapsack of White Privilege." *Independent School*, 1990, 49 (2).

Merriam, S., and Brockett, R. *The Profession and Practice of Adult Education: An Introduction.* San Francisco: Jossey-Bass, 1987.

Moe, J. In B. Cassara, (ed.). *Adult Education in a Multicultural Society.* New York: Routledge, 1990.

Naylor, L. *American Culture: Myth and Reality of a Culture of Diversity.* Westport, Conn.: Bergin & Garvey, 1998.

Novak, M. *Unmeltable Ethnics: Politics & Culture in American Life.* (2nd ed.) New Brunswick, N.J.: Transaction, 1996.

Ogbu, J. "Adaptation to Minority Status and Impact on School Success." *Theory into Practice*, 1992, *31* (4), 287–295.

Quigley, A. B. "Hidden Logic: Reproduction and Resistance in Adult Literacy and Adult Basic Education." *Adult Education Quarterly*, 1990, *40* (2), 103–115.

Ramirez, M., and Castaneda, A. *Cultural Democracy: Bicognitive Development and Education.* New York: Academic Press, 1974.

Ravitch, D. A. "Culture in Common." *Educational Leadership*, 1991, 49 (4), 8–11.

Ross-Gordon, J. M. "Serving Culturally Diverse Populations: A Social Imperative for Adult and Continuing Education." In J. M. Ross-Gordon, L. G. Martin, and Briscoe, B. D. (eds.), *Serving Culturally Diverse Populations.* New Directions for Adult and Continuing Education, no. 49. San Francisco: Jossey-Bass, 1990.

Scheurich, J. "Toward a White Discourse on White Racism." *Educational Researcher, 22* (8), 1993, 5–10.

Sheared, V. "Giving Voice: An Inclusive Model of Interaction—A Womanist Perspective." In *Racism and Sexism in the United States: Fundamental Issues.* New Directions for Adult and Continuing Education, no. 61. San Francisco: Jossey-Bass, 1994.

Tisdell, E. J. *Creating Inclusive Adult Learning Environments: Insights from Multicultural Education and Feminist Pedagogy.* Information Series No. 361. ERIC Clearinghouse on Adult, Career, and Vocational Education, Columbus, Ohio, 1995.

U.S. Bureau of the Census. *Population Projections of the United States by Age, Sex, Race, and Hispanic Origin: 1995–2050.* Washington, DC: U.S. Government Printing Office, 1996.

West, C. *Beyond Eurocentrism and Multiculturalism.* Monroe, Maine: Common Courage Press, 1993.

Williams, R. *Culture and Society, 1780–1950.* New York: Columbia University Press, 1983.

TALMADGE C. GUY is assistant professor in the Department of Adult Education at the University of Georgia, Athens.

2

Theories of adult learning are evolving from individual emphases to the construction of meaning in a social and cultural context.

Adult Learning: Moving Toward More Inclusive Theories and Practices

Donna D. Amstutz

Adult learning theories are often characterized as falling within one of four dominant paradigms: behaviorist, humanist, cognitivist, or liberatory. The first three types have been described as meeting the needs of mainstream economic, academic, and social programs and goals (Welton, 1995). Many of these theories tend to be ahistorical and acontextual. They attempt to explain individualistic ways of knowing and define knowledge as a set of verifiable truths that arise from one culture (usually white, male, and Western-European). These "truths" are then generalized to include "truths" from all other cultures, making the assumption that the "right" way to know things is acceptable only through one hegemonic filter. Briton (1996) describes this view of adult education as "a discursive field that draws on the science of behaviorism, argues for the distinctive nature of the adult learner, posits concepts like 'self-directed' and 'goal-oriented' learning and promotes 'contractual' learning processes and 'facilitated' learning practices" (p. 20).

Liberatory learning theories take into account the history and context of adult learners. Although these theories encourage learners to critically examine the values, beliefs, and assumptions they may have uncritically assimilated from the dominant culture, the implementation of these concepts in adult education practice has been less than stellar. Partly as a result of the often obtuse and difficult language used by many critical theorists, and sometimes as a reaction to the leftist political bent of these theorists, few adult educators have successfully applied these learning theories in their classrooms.

All four views of adult learning often exclude the types of learning that best suit some women, people of color, and people from the working class or those who are unemployed. Other factors that affect adult learning can and should be developed and fostered to promote a more equitable society. This chapter reviews the definitions of knowledge and the assumptions underlying theories of adult learning. It is intended to make explicit the reasons that current adult learning theory may not lead to effective learning for many adults, especially ethnic or racial minorities and women. The chapter concludes with suggestions for ways to teach and learn that more adequately reflect the multiple ways of learning that accommodate the needs of learners in a variety of cultural, ethnic, racial, or economic communities.

Definitions of Knowledge

Most graduate students come to adult education graduate classes with the belief that knowledge emanates from experts. Not infrequently, those students think that the learner's role is to passively absorb subject-matter content and knowledge that is generated by teachers. Many students resist seeing knowledge as a process through which they "weigh their beliefs against a critical examination of alternative possibilities" (Ahlquist, 1992, p. 93). This is partially due to a lack of familiarity with or understanding of different types of knowledge. It also reflects the belief that they—graduate students—cannot produce knowledge themselves.

Knowledge as Objective Truth. From this perspective, *knowledge* is defined as objective truth that is derived from rigorous research. The purpose of research, then, is to identify verifiable facts and to construct valid knowledge that is understood as value-neutral, scientific truth. This perspective reflects the position that the only legitimate knowledge is the knowledge held by people in society who have power. In the United States, legitimate knowledge is constructed primarily from a white, male, Western European perspective. Because adult education is a reflection of this larger societal perspective, it has valued behavioral, individualistic, and cognitive knowledge to the exclusion of other types. This definition of knowledge reflects only one culture, effectively relegating other cultures and types of knowledge to the margins.

Alternative Types of Knowledge. Other types of knowledge are emerging in the adult education literature. *Prescriptive, cultural, fugitive, provisional, ambiguous,* and *subsistence* knowledge, to mention a few, have broadened our understanding of different types of knowledge. Some of these types have very little recognition in mainstream society because they arise from individuals and groups who have very little power.

Cultural knowledge can be defined in one of two ways—either as prescriptive or as emancipatory. Prescriptive cultural knowledge is considered by Bloom (1987) and Hirsch (1987) as that which comes from Western tradition. It is elitist in nature because it specifies knowledge from a particular cultural tradition as better or more important than knowledge from other traditions. Prescriptive cultural knowledge is often touted as objective, scientific knowledge, which hides its true value-laden nature.

Emancipatory cultural knowledge was considered by Freire (1970) and others (Illich, 1970; Heaney, 1995; Horton and Kohl, 1990a) to be intellectual, moral, and contextual understandings constructed by oppressed groups that moved them toward liberatory action. This kind of knowledge is developed by learners toward the goal of taking control of their lives and, through action, changing their environments. Adult learning, from this viewpoint, attempts to provide space for learners who have been marginalized or silenced by the power structures within which they live.

Hill (1995) outlines knowledge that is constructed outside the dominant definition and has therefore escaped the control of society's privileged specialists. His "fugitive" knowledge is constructed in communities that are essentially powerless. He cites informal and formal networking as primary mechanisms for generating and disseminating fugitive knowledge. Thus, fugitive knowledge allows individuals to provide more meaningful representations of themselves. It is often not considered as legitimate or valid knowledge by those who hold power.

Provisional and ambiguous knowledge arise from Hart's (1992) analysis of mother's work. In her view, knowledge is provisional because static knowledge cannot adequately address the continuously changing nature of our work and our lives. Knowledge cannot be finished or absolute because it constantly needs to be created and recreated to reflect changing realities. Hart's view of knowledge is also ambiguous because false dichotomies cannot encompass our interactions. For example, the dichotomies represented by "the role of teacher and the role of student, between authority and obedience, process and content, thought and emotion, self and others, subjectivity and objectivity, empathy and critique, caring and judgment, knowledge and knowledge acquisition, and transforming and submitting to reality" (Hart, 1992, pp. 192–193) represent different value structures. Instead of defining our fixed position relative to any of these dichotomies, our knowledge must shift on a continuum relative to unique learning situations, people, and communities. That is to say, our knowledge must be dynamic and dialectical rather than fixed and static.

Nondichotomous relationships represent wholeness and emphasize the connectedness among people. For example, some adult educators adopt a view of themselves as both learner and teacher. These educators believe they cannot be teachers without also being learners. Conversely, they cannot be learners without also being teachers. Hart goes on to define *subsistence knowing* as knowledge that respects and preserves life through complexity and change and that produces nondominating forms of interaction.

Constructions of various types of knowledge are embedded in adult learning theories. Whose knowledge is validated and whose is excluded is often not made explicit in the way adult learning theories are used. By not examining the types of knowledge inherent in theories, adult educators employ a particular theory of learning that may help maintain and teach knowledge that comes from only one point of view.

Adult Learning Theory

Theories of adult learning can be grouped into several categories. *Instrumental learning* (encompassing cognitive, behavioral, and humanistic theories), *self-directed learning, experiential learning, perspective transformation,* and *situated cognition* are commonly taught and applied in adult education contexts. A brief description of each follows, with identification of the major issues they present to effective learning and teaching in culturally diverse classrooms and marginalized communities.

Instrumental Learning. Instrumental learning theories focus on individual experience. Behavioral, humanistic, and cognitive theories promote individual autonomy as a universal value in adult education and foster the personal growth of individuals. These concepts reflect the emphasis on self and the dominant cultural value of competition in the United States. Both liberal and progressive traditions use instrumental learning for similar purposes such as "the acquisition of knowledge, the development of a rational perspective, and the ability to analyze critically" (Merriam and Brockett, 1997, p. 33). Instrumental learning usually emphasizes specific prescriptive knowledge. In addition to Bloom and Hirsch, the Great Books Foundation institutionalized this approach to adult learning through the Great Books program, which specified content from the Western tradition that was deemed necessary if one is to be knowledgeable. Instrumental learning is often based on the notion of prescriptive cultural knowledge, as previously discussed.

Behavioral learning is a common form of instrumental learning in adult education. It is the basis for instruction in competency-based curricula and programs, governmental and business training programs, and instructional design. Behavioral learning usually results in learning that promotes standardization. Collins (1991) questions the implicit problems that competency- and outcomes-based education causes when he asks, Who determines the competencies and how are they measured? Is it an adult educator's role to specify competencies? The intent of many behavioral programs is to have learners conform to the views, attitudes, and behaviors of the dominant economic and social groups in society. What gives adult educators the right to determine what kinds of competencies people need in order to function in their own communities—communities that often lie outside educators' own experiences in terms of culture, economics, ethnicity, gender, and social roles? Behavioral learning theories use instrumental definitions of knowledge that are often hegemonic. Therefore, cultural or "local" knowledge held by some learners is not recognized as being legitimate.

Humanism also promotes individual development but is more learner-centered. The goal is to produce individuals who have the potential for self-actualization. Learners are characterized as self-directed and internally motivated. Humanism goes beyond behavioral change to changes in values, attitudes, and beliefs about the self. Humanistic learning theories have been prominent in adult education since the early 1920s. Knowles (1980) typified this approach by popularizing the concept of andragogy. However, the exclusion of context and the social mechanisms of constructing meaning and knowledge have limited the applicability of humanistic theories to diverse groups.

A third type of instrumental learning—cognitivism—focuses learning in the mental and psychological processes of the mind, not in behavior. It is concerned with perception, insight, and meaning making and was initially shaped by theorists such as Piaget (1952), Ausubel (1968), and Bruner (1966). Cognitivists focus on examining the mental structures that people construct to provide meaning to information. Learning is inherently individualistic in nature.

Problems of Instrumental Learning Theories. From the perspective of adult education and adult learning that combats racism, sexism, ethnocentrism, and other forms of oppression, there are three major concerns with instrumental learning theories. First, they focus on individual, psychological structures and on processes that are in opposition to the group-oriented, social structures and processes used by some groups (Barr and Birke, 1995). Second, many adult educators misinterpret instrumental learning as comprising all of adult learning (Welton, 1995). Third, these theories are ethnocentric. They are framed from one dominant cultural view that is primarily white, male, and Western European. This one-dimensional view of culture has marginalized the learning approaches of many women, people of color, and members of the working class.

Marginalization occurs when one set of cultural values, assumptions, beliefs, and practices is valued at the sociopolitical and historical expense of other cultural frameworks (Sheared, 1994). As a consequence, there is little room in instrumental learning for fugitive or subsistence knowledge. These types of knowledge, which advocate social interaction as a primary means of building interconnected meanings, lie outside the predominant ways of teaching and learning in adult education. Unlike instrumental learning, fugitive or subsistence knowledge depends on shared histories and understood meanings.

Self-Directed Learning. Self-directed learning has received a great deal of attention in adult learning theory. The concept suggests that adults can plan, conduct, and evaluate their own learning; individuals select the content, the processes, and the outcomes for themselves. Based on assumptions from andragogy (Knowles, 1980), self-directed learning has often been promoted as the goal of adult education. It emphasizes the value of autonomy and individual freedom in learning (Flannery, 1995).

As with the other theories discussed thus far, self-directed learning looks at the individual learner as the primary focus. It fails to take into consideration the social context in which self-directed learning takes place. In addition, it interprets self-directed learning as a method that is more "mature," suggesting that collaborative, cooperative, and other forms of learning are not as potent. Self-directed learning has been criticized as being technicist and competency-based (Collins, 1991).

Experiential Learning. Experiential learning is a way to learn from experience. Adult educators organize experiences in order to facilitate this learning. Progressive education, typified by Lindeman (1926), places value on experience and observation as ways to develop instrumental knowledge. Bruner's (1966) discovery learning and Piaget's (1952) theory of cognitive development both emphasize the primary role of experience in the learning enterprise.

The role of experience has more recently been discussed in relationship to collaborative inquiry (learning) that promotes the "sharing of information in relationships of equality that promotes new growth in each participant (Jackson and MacIsaac, 1994, p. 24). However, experiential learning has also been criticized as focused essentially on developing individual knowledge, thus limiting the social context (Hart, 1992). It often focuses on developing competencies by practicing skills in specific contexts and so can be behavioral in practice.

Perspective Transformation. Perspective transformation is a type of learning in which one's assumptions and beliefs are examined and changed. Mezirow (1990) described it this way:

> [Perspective transformation is] the process of becoming critically aware of how and why our presuppositions have come to constrain the way we perceive, understand, and feel about our world; of reformulating these assumptions to permit a more inclusive, discriminating, permeable, and integrative perspective and of making decisions or otherwise acting upon these new understandings. More inclusive, discriminating, permeable, and integrative perspectives are superior perspectives that adults choose if they can because they are motivated to better understand the meaning of their experience [p. 14].

Welton (1995) critiqued perspective transformation as being within the cognitive-psychological, individualistic tradition of learning theories and not embedded in the social context. Mezirow (1995) answered this criticism by explaining his view that social change begins with individual change. Perspective transformation, then, could be viewed as an individual process that has social implications. But learning that may be collaborative or cooperative is not explained by perspective transformation alone.

Situated Cognition. Situated cognition is a promising theory that treats the context of learning as central for meaning making. Situated cognition, "recognizes the inextricability of thinking and the contexts in which it occurs and exploits the inherent significance of real-life contexts in learning" (Choi and Hannafin, 1995, p. 53). Wilson (1993) summarizes three main assumptions of situated cognition: (1) learning and thinking are social activities; (2) thinking and learning are structured by the tools available in specific situations; and (3) thinking is influenced by the setting in which learning takes place. The concept of "lived experiences" described by feminist (Tisdell, 1995) and womanist (Sheared, 1994) writers has a similar base, which recognizes the centrality of the cultural context in which learning takes place. Situated cognition seems to have a wider view of how learning takes place by adding the context of a learning activity.

Implications for Teaching and Learning

Given the problems with many traditional or mainstream adult learning theories, what are adult educators to do? If mainstream learning theories have shortcomings or do not address the real-world learning needs of women, people of color, or working-class learners, what choices do adult educators have to enhance education for these learners? The central problem is how adult educators can adjust instruction to provide meaningful learning experiences for all learners. Increasing the congruence between learning preferences and needs based on the cultural backgrounds of learners and approaches to teaching and learning employed by adult educators is crucial.

Following are some suggestions as to how adult educators can address the cultural, gender, ethnic, and racial diversity in their classrooms.

• *Help students question theory relative to their own cultural experiences.* Most adult educators acknowledge that adult learners come from widely divergent backgrounds and cultures. Although we may welcome them on a personal level, we often do not know how to reconcile our instruction with the cultures the learners bring to the classroom. Adults bring with them beliefs, values, and understandings that we, as adult educators, may be unfamiliar with. But if we recognize the dissonance formally, we open an opportunity to learn alternative interpretations of theories and practices. When studying a particular theory, we can ask students to reflect on its meaning from their own experiences.

For example, when teaching about the theory and practice of family literacy, I asked students to reflect on their own experiences in relation to literacy in their families. Mainstream adult education suggests that, by increasing the literacy opportunities in the home and by increasing the literacy levels of the adults in the family, the literacy of children will be enhanced. The graduate students, primarily African American and Latino/a, challenged the assumptions on which this theory is based. Most of the learners knew family members or friends who were illiterate. Their personal experiences indicated that the lack of literacy resources in the home and the illiteracy of the adults within them did not hinder their acquisition of literacy skills. They posited that in their community the most important factor in enhancing children's literacy was the *value placed on literacy* by parents and communities. The students created their own fugitive knowledge about family literacy. However, entire adult education programs and millions of federal dollars support the mainstream cultural assumptions that the literacy of parents must be increased in order to help their children become literate.

• *Teach nondichotomous ways of knowing.* Often even critical adult educators fall into the trap of dichotomizing knowledge. Mezirow (1990) argues that dichotomization limits knowledge just as effectively as unexamined cultural canons. He notes: "To set the educational process up as one requiring the learner to share the convictions of the educator's view of social reality (for example, society cast as a simple dichotomy of oppressor vs. oppressed) is indoctrination" (p. 69).

Nondichotomous ways of knowing often are not clear and linear. Barr and Birke (1995) call this type of thinking "a messy, slippery, practical struggle" (p. 129). Because we are uncomfortable with collaboration and conflict in our thinking, our teaching often limits nondichotomous learning. In our classrooms we need to participate in the continuous creation of ideas by encouraging holistic and integrative views that reflect the wholeness of life.

Race and class are not dichotomous factors. White people and people of color are not in either-or categories, that is, either oppressor or oppressed. Separating out people of color or white people as if their experience stands alone misses the way the experiences of all groups are intertwined with those of other groups. Dichotomous factors oversimplify the reality of individuals' lives. Race, for example, is not a singular, defining characteristic. As noted by Andersen and Collins (1995), "All people of color encounter institutional racism, but their actual experiences with racism vary, depending on social class, gender, age, sexuality, and other markers of social position" (p. 63). The same is true for people from different socioeconomic classes as well as for men and women. Individual and group characteristics are not static or unchanging dimensions of learner identity.

• *Seek, acknowledge, and foster alternative forms of knowledge.* Help learners view knowledge as something they can produce. In a graduate class on adult learning theories, I attempted to convey Maslow's hierarchy of needs as an explanation for why adults may or may not participate in adult education activities. My graduate students immediately questioned the theory relative to their own experiences. Even though they all thought the concepts were viable, they were not lived in a hierarchical order. Students created their own graphic depictions of the factors that played into their participation. They added concepts such as community development and cohesiveness that are not emphasized in Maslow's theory. These graphics resembled amoeba-like forms that were not static but fluid. As a professor, my understanding of participation was significantly deepened by my students' knowledge that emerged from their experiences. Adult learners can and do critically assess the assumptions behind culturally assimilated ways of knowing. They can create their own knowledge. Academicians and practitioners need to have an open mind and heart in order to hear and learn from these different types of knowledge.

• *Have the "courage to teach."* Collins (1991) encourages adult educators to resist viewing themselves as only facilitators. Having the courage to teach means that we must recognize and fight the social injustices that pervade our institutions and that create enduring patterns of inequity within them (Goodlad, Soder, and Sirotnik, 1990). For example, acknowledging racism and sexism and pointing out examples of them to our students is a moral dimension of our practice. Antiracist, anticlassist, and antisexist education attempts to reposition Western European cultural perspectives relative to other non-Western cultural perspectives and accounts. The goal of these educational approaches is to reconstruct our knowledge to reflect the interconnectedness of the multiple and diverse voices who created it (Swartz, 1992). A vision of social justice compels us to teach from a broader agenda. Adult educators must identify such perspectives and include them in their curricula.

We must be careful to convey that thinking about race, class, and gender affects experiences of all groups. It is not about studying "victims" or "the other." We should not exclusively focus on women when we discuss gender. Men are important as well. We should include all races, including whites, when we discuss racism. Categories of social experience, race, class, and gender shape all social institutions and systems of meaning. We must not marginalize minority, female, homosexual, and working-class intellectual discourse. We must actively make spaces for these voices to be heard in our classrooms. If we marginalize the voices of minority and feminist scholars, we run the risk of disseminating the same old cultural and political baggage and the same old worldviews. The result is little change in the status of knowledge when the views of culturally marginalized students and scholars are omitted. It is our responsibility to help students identify those societal structures that create and maintain inequality.

• *Use a variety of instructional strategies.* Flannery (1995) cautions, "If adult learning theories promote a classroom that presents the same monocultural environment of language, teaching/learning styles, and communication patterns, and ignores the influence of the social context from which the learners come, failure to learn may well be perpetuated" (p. 155). Most educators teach the way they were taught and were most comfortable learning. This natural tendency is understandable but can be very unproductive with students who learn in a different fashion. Culturally relevant adult education does not necessarily require discomfort on the part of the teacher. However, changing instruction to be more inclusive can be a long-term, intensive process. Several alternative strategies are available. Some examples are *cooperative learning, use of a narrative method,* and *giving voice*; these can be incorporated into our instructional repertoire.

Cooperative learning, which is used extensively in multicultural elementary and secondary education, has potential for adult learning. It provides a collaborative process that purposefully includes the social construction of meaning. It benefits students who value collaboration. Cooperative learning also promotes positive interdependence among learners, is heterogeneous, develops shared leadership skills, and provides tools to help groups process their progress (Slavin, 1990).

Women have used story telling and narratives as strategies for evoking repressed voices in an effort to recover and redefine their roles. Hill-Collins (1990) discusses the use of a narrative method through which people learn. The uses of narratives are "not torn apart in analysis, and [are] trusted as core belief, not admired as science" (p. 312). More recently, Chan (quoted in Medel-Anonuevo, 1997) notes, "In this informal conversational mode, connections, new meaning and understandings emerge through listening, questioning and reflecting on each other's stories, and it is this process that contributes to the recovery of the women's authentic realities as they themselves have experienced them" (p. 88).

Sheared's (1994) suggestion of decentering our instruction and giving voice to learners in our classrooms can be an enlightening experience for both learner and teacher. She delineates four assumptions that guide effective instruction: (1) concrete experience is used as a criterion of meaning; (2) dialogue is the basis for assessing knowledge claims; (3) an ethic of caring emphasizes the uniqueness of individuals, elicits appropriate emotion from the dialogue, and recognizes empathic understanding; and (4) an ethic of personal accountability guides both teaching and learning.

She encourages adult educators to move beyond traditional teaching methods "to limit ourselves to one methodological paradigm risks silencing those to whom we hope to give voice" (p. 35).

• *Construct and maintain supportive learning environments.* Supportive learning environments are necessary to enhance successful participation in our classrooms. Supportive environments are achieved when attention is paid to the furniture (tables and chairs that are conducive to working in small groups as opposed to individual desks that are unusable by people of size and those with disabilities). The learning space should be physically comfortable and free from distractions. A variety of resources should be available for supplementing learning as it is occurring. Tape recorders, portable music boxes, colored markers and paper, tape, and scissors can be very helpful for learners who are visual or auditory learners. These may seem small considerations on first view but can make an immense difference for students who need to "make and see" as they are learning. Adult educators often discuss Gardner's (1983) theory of multiple intelligences but neglect to provide tools for learners who may differ in their approach to learning tasks.

Psychologically supportive environments are also essential. By maintaining the instructional status quo, we are not creating safe environments. People who have been placed in the margins spend much of their emotional and mental resources defending themselves from attacks on their psychic sense of well-being. Gay (1995) notes, "Classrooms are often charged with adversarial opposition, distrust, hostility, discomfort, and tension. Neither students nor teachers can function at their best under these circumstances" (p. 36). We need to learn how to deconstruct mainstream hegemonic assumptions, values, and beliefs embedded in the normative structures and procedures of conventional classroom settings. This requires a thorough understanding of how cultural values shape classroom policies, procedures, and practices. Our adult learning environments must support local practices and languages (Cavanagh, 1997). We need to make the knowledge contained in communities welcome in our classrooms.

- *Continually review educational goals.* Commitments to making teaching more culturally relevant are directly related to one's goals. In Medel-Anonuevo's UNESCO paper, "Learning Gender Justice" (1997), the objectives of instruction should include

Raising the consciousness of men and women concerning gender inequalities and the need to change these unequal relations

Promoting gender-sensitive participatory pedagogy, which acknowledges the daily life experience of women, people of color, and people from all economic circumstances

Adopting policies that enable women, people of color, and the working class to build confidence and developing leadership capacities and management skills

Educating men and women to acknowledge the serious and adverse effects of globalization and hegemonic policies on human beings in all parts of the world, especially on currently marginalized individuals, and communities

Teaching with Love

Apps (1996) describes the impact that love can have on the adult classroom. He came to this position by recognizing that "we have become people of the mind and have forgotten how to also become people of the heart" (p. 27). He goes on to state in his credo, "We believe that our relationship with learners is essential and special and that love and trust are embedded in it" (p. 83). Adult educators need to develop a vision that recognizes caring as important as doing—that caring is a form of action. Building a more positive, inclusive society requires passion, love, and a variety of actions. A part of teaching with love includes being patient with learners who are unconscious of the racism and sexism and ethnocentrism that is embedded in each of us. It also means making our ideologies explicit. We cannot be silent or claim not to have a perspective on issues (Ahlquist, 1992).

hooks (1989) suggests that love also is a crucial component of empowering teaching:

> Love can be and is an important source of empowerment when we struggle to confront issues of sex, race, and class. Working together to identify and

face our difference—to face the ways we dominate and are dominated—to change our actions, we need a mediating force that can sustain us so that we are not broken in the process, so that we do not despair . . . As we work to be loving, to create a culture that celebrates life, that makes love possible, we move against dehumanization, against domination [p. 26].

Conclusion

Adult educators can develop the tools to foster successful learning. As long as we continue to appreciate various knowledges and reflect on our teaching and learning strategies, there is hope that we can provide appropriate, inclusive environments for all learners. "Appreciating diversity cannot wait until the time is right and all conditions are perfect. It must begin now" (Amstutz, 1994, p. 49). We have been challenged before, when Horton and Freire (1990) encouraged us to make the road by walking. Changing the ways we work with learners, through our application of more inclusive learning theories and teaching strategies, will develop not just a road but a freeway into a more equitable future. Teaching of adults must be decentered and transformed at its most fundamental core if we are to be prepared to teach learners who will be more and more racially, culturally, ethnically, socially, economically, and linguistically pluralistic. We have a map. We must begin the journey.

References

Ahlquist, R. "Overcoming Resistance in a Multicultural Foundations Course." In C. Grant, *Research and Multicultural Education: From the Margins to the Mainstream*. Bristol, Penn.: The Falmer Press, 1992.

Amstutz, D. "Staff Development Addressing Issues of Race and Gender." In E. Hayes and S.A.J. Colin III (eds.), *Confronting Racism and Sexism*. New Directions for Adult and Continuing Education, no. 61. San Francisco: Jossey-Bass, 1994.

Andersen, M., and Collins, P. *Race, Class and Gender: An Anthology*. (2nd ed.) Belmont, Calif.: Wadsworth, 1995.

Apps, J. W. *Teaching From the Heart*. Malabar, Fla.: Kreiger, 1996.

Ausubel, D. P. *Educational Psychology: A Cognitive View*. New York: Holt, Rinehart, & Winston, 1968.

Barr, J., and Birke, L. "Cultures and Contexts of Adult Learning: The Case of Women and Science." *Studies in the Education of Adults*, 1995, 27 (2), 119–132.

Bloom, A. *The Closing of the American Mind*. New York: Simon & Schuster, 1987.

Briton, D. *The Modern Practice of Adult Education: A Postmodern Critique*. Albany, N.Y.: State University of New York Press, 1996.

Bruner, J. S. *Toward a Theory of Instruction*. New York: Norton, 1966.

Cavanagh, C. "Adult Learning, Media, Culture, and New Information and Communication Technologies. In UNESCO, *Adult Learning A Key for the 21st Century*. CONFINTEAV Background Papers, Hamburg, Germany, July 14–18, 1997. (ED 410 376)

Choi, J., and Hannafin, M. "Situated Cognition and Learning Environments: Roles, Structures, and Implications for Design." *Educational Technology Research and Development*, 1995, 43 (2), 53–69.

Collins, M. *Adult Education as Vocation: A Critical Role for the Adult Educator*. New York: Routledge, 1991

Flannery, D. "Adult Education and the Politics of the Theoretical Text." In B. Kanpol and P. McLaren (eds.), *Critical Multiculturalism: Uncommon Voices in a Common Struggle.* Westport, Conn.: Bergin & Garvey, 1995.

Freire, P. *Pedagogy of the Oppressed.* New York: Seabury Press, 1970.

Gardner, H. *Frames of Mind.* New York: Basic Books, 1983.

Gay, G. "Building Cultural Bridges: A Bold Proposal for Teacher Education." In F. Schultz (ed.), *Multicultural Education 95/96.* The Annual Editions Series. Guilford, Conn.: Dushkin, 1995.

Goodlad, J., Soder, R., and Sirotnik, K. (eds.). *The Moral Dimensions of Teaching.* San Francisco: Jossey-Bass, 1990.

Hart, M. *Working and Educating for Life: Feminist and International Perspectives on Adult Education.* New York: Routledge, 1992.

Heaney, T. *Issues in Freirean Pedagogy.* Internet http//nlu.nl.edu/ace/Resources/Documents/FreireIssues.html, 1995.

Hill, R. J. "Learning to Transgress: A Sociohistorical Conspectus of the American Gay Lifeworld as a Site of Struggle and Resistance." *Studies in the Education of Adults,* 1995, *28* (2), 253–279.

Hill-Collins, P. "The Social Construction of Black Feminist Thought." In M. Malson, E. Mudimbe-Boyi, J. O'Barr, and M. Wyer (eds.), *Black Women in America: Social Science Perspectives.* Chicago: University of Chicago Press, 1990.

Hirsch, E. D., Jr. *Cultural Literacy: What Every American Needs to Know.* New York: Houghton Mifflin, 1987.

hooks, b. *Talking Back, Thinking Feminist, Thinking Black.* Boston, Mass: South End Press, 1989.

Horton, M., and Freire, P. *We Make the Road by Walking.* Philadelphia, Penn.: Temple University Press, 1990.

Horton, M., Kohl, J., and Kohl, H. *The Long Haul: An Autobiography.* New York: Doubleday, 1990.

Illich, I. *Deschooling Society.* New York: Harper Collins, 1970.

Jackson, L., and MacIsaac, D. "Introduction to a New Approach to Experiential Learning." In L. Jackson and R. S. Caffarella (eds.), *Experiential Learning: A New Approach.* New Directions for Adult and Continuing Education, no. 62. San Francisco: Jossey-Bass, 1994.

Knowles, M. S. *The Modern Practice of Adult Education: From Pedagogy to Andragogy.* (2nd ed.) New York: Cambridge Books, 1980.

Lindeman, E. C. *The Meaning of Adult Education.* New York: New Republic, 1926.

Medel-Anonuevo, C. "Learning Gender Justice: The Challenge for Adult Education in the 21st Century." In UNESCO, *Adult Learning: A Key for the 21st Century.* CONFINTEAV Background Papers, Hamburg, Germany, July 14–18, 1997. (ED 410 376)

Merriam, S., and Brockett, R. *The Profession and Practice of Adult Education: An Introduction.* San Francisco: Jossey-Bass, 1997.

Mezirow, J. "Transformation Theory of Adult Learning." In M. Welton (ed.), *In Defense of the Lifeworld Critical Perspectives on Adult Learning.* Albany, N.Y.: State University of New York Press, 1995.

Mezirow, J., and Associates. *Fostering Critical Reflection in Adulthood: A Guide to Transformative and Emancipatory Education.* San Francisco: Jossey-Bass, 1990.

Piaget, J. *The Language and Thought of the Child.* London: Routledge and Kegan-Paul, 1952.

Sheared, V. "Giving Voice: An Inclusive Model of Instruction—A Womanist Perspective." In E. Hayes and S.A.J. Colin III (eds.), *Confronting Racism and Sexism.* New Directions for Adult and Continuing Education, no. 61. San Francisco: Jossey-Bass, 1994.

Slavin, R. E. *Cooperative Learning: Theory, Research, and Practice.* Englewood Cliffs, N.J.: Prentice Hall, 1990.

Swartz, E. "From a Compensatory to a Scholarly Foundation." In Grant, C. (ed.), *Research and Multicultural Education: From the Margins to the Mainstream.* Bristol, Penn.: The Falmer Press, 1992.

Tisdell, E. J. *Creating Inclusive Adult Learning Environments: Insights from Multicultural Education and Feminist Pedagogy*. Columbus, Ohio: ERIC Clearinghouse on Adult, Career, and Vocational Education, Series No. 361, 1995.

Welton, M.(ed.). *In Defense of the Lifeworld: Critical Perspectives on Adult Learning*. Albany, N.Y.: State University of New York, 1995.

Wilson, A. L. "The Promise of Situated Cognition." In S. B. Merriam (ed.), *An Update on Adult Learning Theory*. New Directions for Adult and Continuing Education, no. 57. San Francisco: Jossey-Bass, 1993.

DONNA D. AMSTUTZ is associate professor of adult education at the University of Wyoming and director of the Wyoming Literacy Resource Center.

3

Giving voice in adult basic education classes to the polyrhythmic realities of African American adult learners and teachers will allow both to see reflections of their shared history, language, race, and gender.

Giving Voice: Inclusion of African American Students' Polyrhythmic Realities in Adult Basic Education

Vanessa Sheared

In the movie *Field of Dreams,* the main character, the son of Joe Shula of the famous 1906 Chicago White Sox, built a baseball field in the corn fields of Iowa. Referring to a corn field as a possible baseball field, one of the characters in the film says, "If you build it, they will come." The idea behind this simple statement is that if you make the place you are inviting people to visit accessible, meaningful, and convenient, then they will come. You only need to make it possible. In the film, once the baseball field was completed, the 1906 White Sox baseball team materialized and played a game. The son of Joe Shula had built a place in which the 1906 White Sox might play one final game. More important for the story line, however, was that Joe Shula played for the White Sox and that this was the first and only time the son had an opportunity to meet his father and watch him play baseball.

The moral that educators can draw from this story is that we must create programs that allow students to employ their beliefs, values, and lived experiences in the classroom. By doing so, students will not only attend adult education programs, but they will stay in those programs until they have achieved their goals as well as the programs' goals. Additionally, for African Americans, who have not participated in adult programs as much as other racial and language groups, it is critical that we examine why that is true.

I believe that by creating program environments that are welcoming and reflective of their needs, we can attract African American adult learners who are more likely to attend and stay in adult education programs. By making learners' race, gender, and language experiences a part of the curriculum in adult basic education (ABE) classes, African American learners can began to see reflections of themselves. This then will increase their motivation to come and complete their educational programs.

As adult educators we can also use the baseball analogy to raise some important questions concerning what we can do for the African American ABE student. For instance, we should ask ourselves the following questions: (1) Are curriculum materials available to work with African American adult learners in ABE classes reflective of their history, culture, language and experiences?; (2) Does the classroom environment reflect the African American learners' educational needs?; (3) What role models, if any, are being used to reflect the African American learners' realities?; and (4) What are we as adult educators doing for or providing African American learners that will encourage them to participate in ABE programs? These questions are only examples of what we need to take into consideration with this population, if we want them to participate.

Factors Affecting ABE Program Planners

Practitioners seeking answers to these questions face three important considerations: (1) little research has been done to determine whether ABE programs are inclusive; (2) funding for more research is insufficient; and (3) the children of potential applicants are a factor. I will discuss these problems in the sections to follow; each has been given as a reason for limited or nonparticipation in adult basic education (ABE) programs by African American adults.

Research. With the exception of a handful of analyses (Briscoe and Ross, 1991; Colin, 1989; Colin and Preciphs, 1991; Guy, 1999; Ihle, 1990; Rachal, 1986; Sheared, 1994b; Valentine and James, 1993), few adult education studies have addressed the issue of race and gender in planning programs for African American learners. Although there is literature (Brookfield, 1986; Collard and Stalker, 1991; Hayes, 1989; Hayes and Colin, 1994; Knowles, 1980; Boone, 1985; Caffarella, 1994) on designing programs for adult learners in various settings, there has been limited focus outside the aforementioned that address race or gender in program planning. Given what has been written, we are led to ask, Will African American adults in need of basic education classes be adequately served using the current program design models?

Funding. The insufficient funding available for program and curriculum development in ABE programs creates short- and long-term problems in identifying adequate curricular and instructional resources to meet African American learners' needs (Sheared, 1994a). With no clear guidance from the literature and with insufficient funding for research by practitioners and for sharing of information within practitioner networks, the problems facing ABE programs that serve African American adults are almost overwhelming. Given the lack of funding for programs designed for African Americans in ABE, which has led to limited participation, I believe it is critically important to discuss the significance of race, gender and class as it affects this population.

The Children. It has been stated that the reason many African American adults attend ABE programs is their children. Many adults have difficulties reading and writing and are unable to help their children with these skills. Consequentially, many adults come to ABE classes to improve on these skills so they can help their children. They often view ABE classes as a way to fulfill their goals, as well as a way to help prepare their children for the future. Although this might be an initial motivating factor, it may not be enough to sustain their participation.

In addition to the multiple personal, social, and economic factors that might interfere with adults' continued participation in adult education activities, we as adult educators bring a host of factors that affect learners' participation in ABE programs. We are often unable to clearly reflect our own experiences and philosophies as they affect adult learners. Our experiences and philosophy are grounded in our understanding of how we view ourselves in terms of race, gender, language, and class and in how we view the teacher-student relationship. As we begin to reflect on our role as educators and on the ways our role intersects with our race, gender, language, and class, we can then begin to address the needs of our students as they relate to these factors. More important, we can begin to see how these factors affect our philosophy and our practice.

Most adult educators have a philosophy that reflects their experience and knowledge but have not necessarily given much thought to how their philosophy affects their practice. Nor do educators necessarily give much thought to how their race, gender, class, or language influences their philosophy and what they do in the classroom.

This philosophical problem can be partially attributed to the fact that the adult education field has more than one definition, descriptor, or perspective (Beder, 1989; Darkenwald and Merriam, 1982; Merriam and Brockett, 1997). Although some would argue that this is good, others would say that it creates problems on many levels. Having many definitions is not necessarily bad, for it can lead to the development and implementation of strategies that work with a broad spectrum of people. However, the lack of a clear definition can lead to a stop-gap approach to programming for at-risk populations, as African Americans have often been labeled. This argument is important, but I will address it only as it relates to how we work with African American learners in ABE classes.

The field of adult education is built on a foundation of theoretical paradigms that encompass psychology, sociology, philosophy, anthropology, history, and education. All of these disciplines address some element of the human condition and represent perspectives that we need to understand as teachers working in the classroom. For instance, the field of psychology informs us about an individual's emotional and cognitive development. Sociology informs us about how individuals relate to their community and environment. And education provides educators with a vehicle to aid learners through the learning process. I believe the field of adult education combines all these elements.

Andragogy

A term that has often been used to distinguish adult education from education for children to adults is *andragogy*. This term was popularized in the United States during the early 1970s by Knowles (1980). Since his use of this term in the field of adult education, adult educators in the United States have used it to describe the way one should teach adults as opposed to children. So *andragogy* is defined as the art and science of teaching adults, and *pedagogy* is defined as the art and science of teaching children. Both terms suggest a way of viewing and addressing the needs of learners within the learning environment.

Although andragogy seems to provide us with a way to describe what we do, the term has also been the subject of much debate and critique (see Merriam, 1993; Cross, 1981). Andragogy calls our attention to the primacy of learners' experience, which shapes current learning needs. Andragogy directs our attention to identifying current learning needs and using learners' experience to help meet those needs. One main problem with using this philosophy to address African American adult learners in ABE programs is that it presupposes that one's experiences are grounded in the vocational and social as opposed to race, gender, and class. Such misconceptions can result in the development of programs that "turn the learners off" in the learning environment.

Polyrhythmic Realities

I introduced the concept of polyrhythmic realities (Sheared 1994a) to the field of adult education in order to highlight the complexity of learners' lived experiences. The intersection of race, gender, and class is essential to this concept. The lived experiences of learners and teachers are grounded in how they view themselves in relation to these factors. Specifically, African American learners' lived experience must be viewed as a shifting spiral that interconnects to the African American learners' culture, race, gender, and class. As this shift occurs, issues of oppression and privilege begin to surface and must be addressed before the way they interact with the teacher or other learners in the learning environment can be changed.

Consequently, a main difference between andragogy and the concept of polyrhythmic realities is that the term *andragogy* focuses on the life experiences, whereas the term *polyrhythmic realities* refers to the students' lived experience within a sociocultural, political, and historical context.

In practical terms, this means that students' and teachers' race, class, and gender are included and examined in curriculum structure and delivery. This strategy includes developing an understanding and appreciation of both the students' and the teachers' personal, economic, political, and historical lived experiences. This means that if we want to recruit and retain African American adults in ABE classrooms, we must begin to analyze our own motivations, perspectives, and philosophical assumptions about teaching and learning. If learners can see their culture and history contributing to their political and economic standing, then I contend that they will begin to value their role in the learning process as well as in their communities and society. The connection between race, class, gender, historical and sociocultural and political realities, then, is essential if we intend to build programs that will not only draw students into them but will keep them until they have achieved their goals.

The question that practitioners must answer as they design programs for African American adult learners is, How can learners' lived experiences be brought into the curriculum? Answers to this question could lead to the development of programs that not only attract African Americans to their programs but keep them there. Moreover, attention needs to be given to earlier educational influences (Quigley, 1990, 1992) and the lack of selfethnic reflectors (Colin, 1989) as they contribute to African American participation in adult basic education programs and classrooms.

Factors Influencing Retention of African Americans in ABE Classrooms

ABE programs' emphasis on serving African Americans is often viewed as a marginal concern for program administrators, given that they have to service all adults in a given community. The attention that can be given to this is often predicated on the type of funding that is allocated to adult programming either in or for African American or other communities (Sheared, 1992).

Even though attention has been given to why some adults do not participate in adult education programs, these studies (Darkenwald and Scanlan, 1984; Darkenwald and Gavin, 1987; Darkenwald and Valentine, 1986; Fisher, 1986; Kopka and Peng, 1993) fail to address the effect of race, class, and gender on participation. Although the studies are helpful and provide us with a general framework for understanding the participation of adults in ABE programs, they do not address the ways race, class, and gender issues affect the participation rates of African Americans in ABE classes. I believe that attention to these issues is necessary if adult educators are to increase African American adult participation and matriculation in ABE programs.

Connecting Learning to Lived Experiences. In a study conducted in 1994 concerning the participation of African Americans in California's ABE's classrooms, I found that participation occurred as a result of ABE practitioners putting forth efforts to include African Americans in their programs, institutions making it a priority in their policies and in the funding allocated to this population, and students believing that their histories, culture, and perspectives mattered to those in charge of the program.

The pervasive theme that surfaced in this study was that African Americans tended to participate when they "connected" with the teacher, the students, and the program goals. Moreover, the acknowledgment of one's cultural reality or lived experience was a critical factor. Students who found that their lived experiences were acknowledged by the program staff, teachers, and administrators not only participated, they persisted. Those who did not connect with the goals and purpose of the adult education program because their real or felt needs were not met did not continue. Or if they started attending the program, they stopped once they recognized that the aims and goals of the program did not meet their need. In this study the students' need to connect what they did in the classroom to their lived experience appeared to have been an important factor.

Valuing Education. ABE practitioners must remember that African Americans have always valued education, as evidenced by the slaves who risked their lives to learn how to read. Even though African Americans have overcome many obstacles, they also understand that obtaining an education alone does not mean that they will automatically obtain equity and equality in the workforce. Adult education programs must recognize this and provide African American adults with clear and realistic options based on their understanding of the role racism, sexism, and other "isms" play in the lived experiences of their students.

Recognizing That Students Matter. Furthermore, teachers must recognize that African Americans place value on education and knowledge and that it is important for them to believe that they matter and to believe that what they learn will be used to move them forward economically. We must remember, however, that even though some have given up on formal education as the arena through which they will move forward, it does not mean they do not value learning. Learning is viewed quite differently for some, as noted in this student's comments: "I discovered that even with finishing the reading and writing process it wasn't enough for me to get to the workforce. So I started going to a more advanced adult training. . . . I came back to adult school so I could get my diploma and I could go to college and get ahead" (interview conducted in April 1992 concerning the participation of African Americans in Adult Basic Education Programs in California).

Relevance. Students—African Americans in particular—need to see that what they are doing in school will have some relevance to what they do in the workforce and at home. This means that learning for learning's sake is not a sufficiently strong motivation for most African American adult learners to participate in ABE programs. Because economic factors, family pressures and constraints, and environmental factors place significant pressures on potential learners, they need to know that what they are doing will have a positive impact on these concerns. The learning environment and the relationships students establish with teachers and with each other also become critical factors in their decision to participate in ABE programs.

Experiences. The political and sociocultural experiences of African Americans in history are also factors that practitioners need to recognize. Throughout history, legislation has been sought and enacted so that African Americans could gain access and equity in education and in the workforce. Bell (1987) concludes in *And We Are Not Saved* that even though legislation was passed to redress racial imbalance in education as well as job opportunities, as a group African Americans have not moved very far, even though some individuals have done quite well. Although the gains made in these areas have benefited some, he asks us to look at this more critically. We as a nation should ask ourselves, Why is it that for some Americans legislation is needed in order for them to obtain equity and equality in our society and for others it is a given right because of the color of their skin?

Testing. Adult educators must also recognize the ways in which academic achievement and test scores influence their interactions with their students. For instance the gap in educational gains reflected in the National Adult Literacy Survey (NALS) suggests that African Americans do not value education. According to NALS, African Americans represent approximately 11 percent of the total population in the United States, and a significant number of them have failed to go beyond 11.6 years of schooling (NCES, 1994). In comparison, European Americans represent 76 percent and remain in school on average 12.8 years. Latino and Asian–Pacific Islanders represent 10 percent and 2 percent, and on average they complete 10.6 and 13.0 years of school respectively. Asians or Pacific Islanders complete 13.0 years, and Native Americans or Alaskan Natives complete an average of 11.7 years of schooling. The only group with fewer years in school than African Americans was Hispanics, who remain in school on average for 10.6 years. Although these numbers appear to contradict the fact that African Americans value education and learning, one must look closer and ask why is it that this group who fought to gain the rights to attend school are now not participating? What's wrong with this picture? Moreover, when they are given a second chance to gain an education through adult basic education programs, why aren't they participating in larger numbers?

Including Polyrhythmic Realities. In order for adult education practitioners to fully grapple with the polyrhythmic realities of African American adults, as well as other groups identified as minorities, they must begin to examine the literature on race, gender, and class in adult education literature and educational literature in general. Furthermore, ABE practitioners must examine literature that critically reflects their own language, race, gender, and class, as well as other factors that might influence or contribute to how they teach to these groups of learners.

Given that the primary concern of this chapter is African American men and women, both an Africentric and an Africentric feminist perspective will be applied to analyzing the reasons African Americans continue to participate in adult basic education classes. As we begin to employ concepts and perspective in the curriculum that reflect the lived experiences of adult learners, we should begin to see changes in who participates. I now turn to ways in which adult basic educators can begin to use this lens to examine and construct curricula for African American learners.

Giving Voice. Teachers must give voice to learners' lived experiences. They must acknowledge the significance of race, gender, and class in the learning environment. Giving voice to learners' lived experience should help learners acquire the skills and tools they need, not only to move forward economically but to challenge the status quo. If they understand how their past, present, and future are affected by lived experiences, they can begin to change the ways they confront institutional, situational, or dispositional barriers in their everyday lives.

Adult educators must examine the ways in which race, class, gender, and the political and sociocultural realities intersect and influence participation. These questions should be asked and answered by practitioners as they develop programs for African American adult learners.

Uncovering Polyrhythmic Realities

The concept of polyrhythmic realities offers adult educators an alternative way to think about how to address the effects of race, class, and gender in the classroom environment. Drawing on the Africentric epistemological perspective of Hill-Collins (1990) I began to look for ways I could creatively teach and address issues of race, class, and gender in the classroom. Although the model she proposed was initially aimed at collecting data from marginalized groups by using the narrative method, I saw this as a way to address the lived experiences of adult learners in the classroom.

A Different Way of Knowing. The method involves an acknowledgment of a way of knowing that is not grounded in Western linear traditions. Africentric feminist epistemology attempts to provide a medium through which one's interpretation of behavior and thought is grounded in the history, culture, economics, race, gender, language, sexual orientation, and religion of those involved in the research. According to Hill-Collins, "Africanists' analyses of the Black experience generally agree on the fundamental elements of an Afrocentric standpoint" (p. 307). She further states that their shared Africentric values permeate their family structure, religious institutions, culture, and community life in all its variations. It is a distinct way of knowing that permeates the African diaspora.

It is the intersection of these positions or realities that ultimately affects the way a person interprets, speaks, and reads the word and the world. *Womanism* is a term that describes this intersection. The term was introduced by Alice Walker and is one that I subscribe to as a way to validate the African American woman's and man's standpoint and at the same time acknowledge other people's standpoints. The womanist perspective is distinct from the feminist perspective in that it acknowledges the distinguishing effects of race, class, gender, and other "isms." The feminist perspective acknowledges the distinguishing effects of gender and class only. Although gender and class issues affect European American women, African American women, Asian American women, Native American women, Latina women—all women—at different times, each woman has distinct understandings of the issues. Hill-Collins concludes, "Since Black women have access to both the Afrocentric and the feminist standpoints, an alternative epistemology used to rearticulate a Black woman's standpoint reflects elements of both traditions" (p. 308). Although these perspectives are not mutually exclusive, it is important to note that the womanist perspective emphasizes the intersection of multiple realities.

These multiple realities are interwoven into a unifying whole. They contradict yet complement each other—that is, they are nondichotomous. They are intersecting and interwoven points of reality—they are polyrhythmic. In other words, an individual's experiences can be described as simultaneously intersecting realities. Figure 3.1 reflects the intersecting yet simultaneous realities of the African American adult learner. The "you" in the middle represents the student or teacher and is centered to reflect the ways in which race, class, gender, and language affect how one sees oneself and how one should be perceived as the instructor or student (depending on the perspective) in the learning environment.

Polyrhythmic is a term used by some Africanists to reflect the aesthetic essence of African art, music, dance, and language. It refers to the interconnections between race, class, gender, and language that allow them to read, write, and interpret the written and oral word. It ultimately induces a sense of self-understanding and self-worth, which is reflected in one's words and thoughts. An understanding of these multiple standpoints—polyrhythms—helps one determine what is required to survive in an unfamiliar yet sometimes racist and sexist environment. The model represents the intersecting polyrhythmic realities based upon the Africentric feminist deconstruction of an individual's worldview.

Figure 3.1. Polyrhythmic Realities

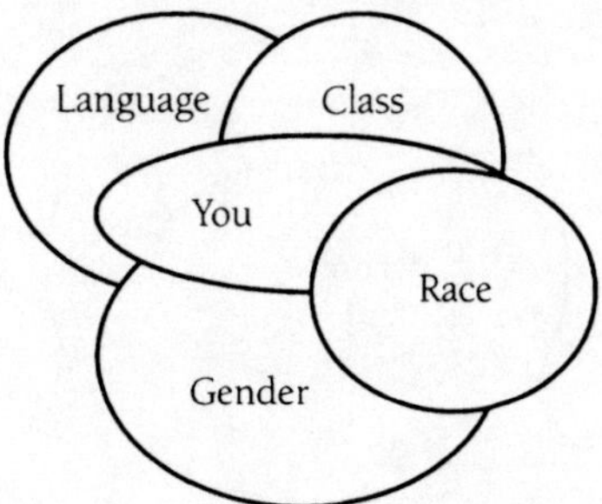

Use of Dialogue. Dialogue is essential to being able to give voice to learners' experiences. It is key to uncovering and discovering the ways in which race, gender, class, and language have played a role in African American adult learners' ability to succeed in the learning environment. *Gumba ya ya* is a term used by Tisch (Barkeley-Brown, 1990) that means *everybody talking at once*; it is a metaphor that can be used to describe the ways many people dialogue in their homes. Students talking to students while the teacher is talking is an example; it is often viewed as disrespectful and for many can be distracting, but these mini-conversations can often lead to students gaining a better understanding of the subject matter when they are used to aid the learning process. As a result, these dialogues can help students gain a greater appreciation for each other as well as the instructor.

Another aspect of dialogue is the call and response. (The call and response is a communicative interaction between a speaker and the audience. The audience responds with verbal signs of understanding and affirmation.) The call and response evokes a sense of caring for self and others. When given an opportunity to explore lived experiences, as well as the curriculum content simultaneously, students can begin to gain confidence in their ability and desire to learn individually and collectively. Ultimately, engaging in dialogue can help students uncover and discover their polyrhythmic realities within the learning environment.

In order to give voice in the classroom, teachers must be willing to relinquish some of their perceived power and control over the learning environment. It is perceived power and control, because it is often given to them as a function of their role in that setting. Their race, gender, language, or class can either increase or decrease the power and control that they have. Aronowitz and Giroux (1985) refer to the exercising of power and control over others as hegemony—"a process of continuous creation and includes the constant structuring of consciousness" (p. 88). Moreover, it happens "systematically through and within the educational, political, social and cultural arenas" (Sheared, 1992). (See Figure 3.2.)

Hegemony leads to silence and eliminates the student's voice. In order to give voice to students, the teacher must (1) acknowledge his or her per-

Figure 3.2.

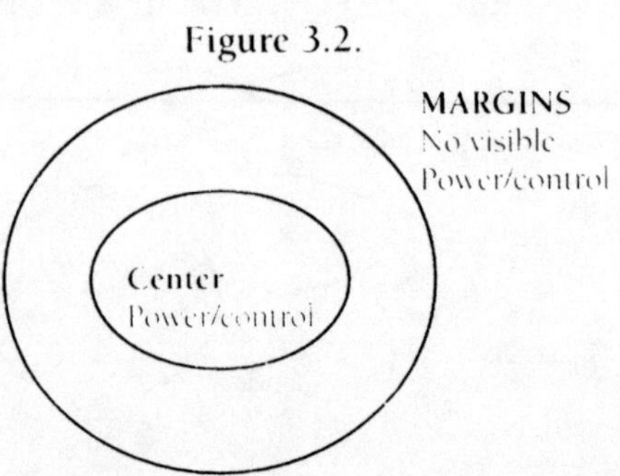

ceived power and control in the classroom; (2) be willing to examine how their race, class, gender have either privileged them or oppressed them; (3) be willing to share power and control within the learning environment; and (4) create space for their students' histories and cultures, as well as their own, to be examined as they relate to learning. Hegemony requires that the teacher understand his or her own polyrhythmic realities and provide students with opportunities to explore their own realities.

To give voice, then, means that the teacher understands that even though he or she is currently operating from a position of power and control while in the classroom, that is only temporal control over students, who are viewed as being in the margin. Even though the students are in the margin, they are not operating solely from a marginalized standpoint. Learners also have ways of exercising power, both in and outside of the learning environment. For example, learners can challenge teachers, resist learning, and reject the class. In order for voice to be acquired, the teacher and students must take responsibility for what is learned and how it is learned in the classroom.

It must also be understood that giving voice is not divorced from content; rather, giving voice promotes an understanding of content and seeks to underscore its significance in determining whose knowledge gets heard and acknowledged in the discourse. Giving voice means that the teacher moves from the center into the margin. Students are given an opportunity to share their understandings of the word and the world through dialogue. As students and the teacher engage in the call and response, students gradually begin to take responsibility for reading and interpreting the word. They slowly begin to understand that they are the authors of their own histories, cultures, languages, and economics. It is through the shifting of margins and centers that learners and teacher begin to uncover their realities with one another.

As teachers and students participate in giving voice to each other, they begin to recognize and share power and control over what and how knowledge is explored and analyzed within the learning environment. In a class that I conducted on adult learning, students were asked to interpret what *giving voice* meant, based on their examination of their polyrhythmic realities (Sheared, 1996). They concluded that giving voice allowed one to

Engage in dialogue with each other as colearners and coauthors of knowledge production and infusion

Define silencing and examine how it occurs, as well as the ultimate impact it has on an individual's thinking and feeling, both in and outside of the learning environment

Recognize, respect, and encourage individuality through empathetic understanding; race, class, gender, language, as well as other contributing factors being seen as intersecting points of being and knowing

Understand that universal norms are ever-changing factors that are influenced by history, politics, and socioeconomic realities and acknowledge the commonality of their needs, ideas, and to appreciate that humanness evolves as one begins to place the universal norms and individual realities within a community context of "wholeness"

Explore connectedness as commonalities and explore and recognize that this contributes to an increased understanding of their multiple and intersecting realities

Eliminate or decrease stereotyping, as students begin to see each other as individuals who are connected by their common universals but who have different experiences and understandings of those experiences

Allow individual and community consciousness to evolve as the individual begins to see himself or herself connected through convergent and divergent realities and begin exploring ways to change not only themselves but understand their responsibility for participating in change that builds communities that are accepting of these varying realities

The extent to which the preceding events occur within the learning environment depends on whether students and teacher allow themselves to speak and empathetically listen to each other.

Conclusion

Adult educators refer to the education of adults as andragogy. The use of this term to describe adult learning suggests the need to explore and use the experiences of adults when engaged in providing educational opportunities for them. Life experience is viewed as one of many factors that contribute to the way adults process and use knowledge in the learning environment. Andragogy differentiates adults' reasons for learning from children's reasons for learning. Adults are problem-centered, whereas children are subject-centered. Adults are self-directed and know what they need to learn, whereas children are other-directed and rely on others to determine what needs to be learned.

Although the concept of andragogy provides us with a paradigm for differentiating between adult and childhood learning, it fails to acknowledge the polyrhythmic realities of the learners. African American adults' lived experiences are grounded in race, class, gender, and other cultural factors that can contribute to their understanding of the process for producing knowledge.

The womanist perspective provides a framework for understanding the polyryhthmic realities of the learners within the learning environment. Even though multiculturalists acknowledge culture and its effect on learning, they often tend to compartmentalize the learner's experiences into cultural norms rather than examine them with regard to race, class, and gender. Teachers often view oppression as that which affects only minorities, not those privileged by race, gender, or class. Cultural experiences are the only ones that educators examine within and outside of the learning environment. However, I would argue that we must go beyond the "cultural" and we must acknowledge and include factors like race, gender, class, and language into the curriculum frameworks. We must include the ways in which these factors intersect with the sociocultural, political, and historical realities of both the students and the teachers. In order to do this, adult education practitioners will have to reexamine and articulate their philosophies about their role as teachers, their students' roles as learners, and the role of the learning environment and community on learning.

For ABE programs serving African American students, giving voice means that learners' lived experiences are made a central part of the narrative discourse that occurs both in the classroom and throughout the curriculum.

According to Sheared (1994a), our goal as adult educators is to

> find ways in which we can uncover and acknowledge the voice of each student, to recognize that we, like our students bring polyrhythmic realities to the learning environment; to find ways of disempowering ourselves in the learning environment so that students begin to take responsibility for their learning. Moreover, we must understand that the information we proffer is grounded in a political, social, historical, sexual, racial and economical context and, that it is unique to us [p. 31].

In other words, we must recognize that our subjective understanding of the world is different yet interconnected with our students' understanding.

Giving voice requires an acknowledgment that knowledge is inherently political and serves to socialize and condition behavior. Norms that often negate the voices of those who lack power and control over the discourse must therefore be reassessed and analyzed, by both teacher and students. This means that adult educators must formally acknowledge their inherent domination over the students and the knowledge that is introduced to the learner. Together, they should engage in an examination of how their lived experiences affect the way they read, speak, and interpret the word and the world. The reexamination of universality and polyrhythmic realities will provide the educator and the learner with opportunities for interpreting knowledge based on a reconceptualization of "what was and what is."

Giving voice clearly provides the learner and teacher with an opportunity to communicate their oppositional worldview. An understanding of these worldviews is essential to the interpretation of how their educational, political, historical, and social realities contribute to creating adult learning communities. Giving voice promotes connectedness while acknowledging the inherent uniqueness of the learner as well as the facilitator.

The Africentric perspective allows adult educators to reframe and reexamine knowledge and truth in relation to its sociohistorical, political, and economic antecedents. It is clear that if educators of African American adult learners are going to use the experiences of the learners to foster learning, then we must begin reframing and reconceptualizing the way we view both ours as well as the students' experiences. Finally, we must seek ways to shift the center and the margins so that learners' and instructors' experiences can be reexamined to determine the degree to which each one of us contributes to our own as well as the learners' education or miseducation. In so doing, we will begin to design programs that should bring students in and keep them there until they have achieved their academic goals.

References

Aronowitz, S., and Giroux, H. *Education Under Siege: The Conservative, Liberal, and Radical Debate Over Schooling.* South Hadley, Mass. Bergin & Garvey, 1985.

Barkeley-Brown, E. "African American Women's Quilting. A Framework for Conceptualizing and Teaching African American Women's History." In M. Malson, E. Mudimbe-Boyi, J. O. Barr, and M. Wyer (eds.), *Black Women in America: Social Science Perspectives.* Chicago: University of Chicago Press, 1990.

Beder, H. "Purposes and Philosophies of Adult Education." In S. B. Merriam and P. M. Cunningham (eds.), *Handbook of Adult and Continuing Education.* San Francisco: Jossey-Bass, 1989.

Bell, D. *And We Are Not Saved: The Elusive Quest for Racial Justice.* New York: Basic Books, 1987.

Boone, E. J. *Developing Programs in Adult Education.* Prospect Heights, Ill.: Waveland Press, 1985.

Briscoe, D. B., and Ross, J. M. *Racial and Ethnic Minorities and Adult Education.* In S. B. Merriam and P. M. Cunningham (eds.), *Handbook of Adult and Continuing Education.* San Francisco: Jossey-Bass, 1989.

Brookfield, S. D. *Understanding and Facilitating Adult Learning: A Comprehensive Analysis of Principles and Effective Practices.* San Francisco: Jossey-Bass, 1986.

Caffarella, R. *Planning Programs for Adult Learners: A Practical Guide for Educators, Trainers, and Staff Developers.* San Francisco: Jossey-Bass, 1994.

Colin, S.A.J., III. "Cultural Literacy: Ethnocentrism versus Selfethnic Reflectors." *Thresholds in Education,* Nov., 1989.

Colin, S.A.J., III, and Preciphs, T. K. "Perceptual Patterns and the Learning Environment: Confronting White Racism." In R. Hiemstra (ed.), *Creating Environments for Effective Adult Learning.* New Directions for Adult Continuing Education, no. 50. San Francisco: Jossey-Bass, 1991.

Collard, S., and Stalker, J. "Women's Trouble: Women, Gender and the Learning Environment." In R. Hiemstra (ed.), *Creating Environments for Effective Adult Learning.* New Directions for Adult and Continuing Education, no. 50. San Francisco: Jossey-Bass, 1991.

Cross, K. P. *Adults as Learners: Increasing Participation and Facilitating Learning.* San Francisco: Jossey-Bass, 1981.

Darkenwald, G. G., and Gavin, W. J. "Dropout as a Function of Discrepancies Between Expectations and Actual Experiences of the Classroom Social Environment." *Adult Education Quarterly,* 1987, 37, 152–163.

Darkenwald, G. G., and Merriam, S. *Adult Education: Foundations of Practice.* New York: Harper & Row, 1982.

Darkenwald, G. G., and Valentine, T. "Measuring the Social Environment of Adult Education Classrooms." Proceedings of the Adult Education Research Conference, no. 27. Syracuse, N.Y.: Syracuse University, 1986.

Fisher, J. "Participation in Educational Activities by Older Adults." *Adult Education Quarterly,* 1986, 36, 202–210.

Gordon, L., and Gordon, C. (producers). Robinson, P. A. (Screenwriter). *Field of Dreams* [Film]. Hollywood: Universal City Studios, 1989.

Guy, T. C. "Culturally Relevant Literacy Instruction for African American Adults: African American English (AAE) as an Instructional Resource for Teachers of African American Adults." In D. Ntiri (ed.), *Pedagogy for Adult Learners: Methods and Strategies.* Vol. 2: *Models for Adult and Lifelong Learning.* Detroit: Office of Adult and Lifelong Learning Research, Wayne State University, 1999.

Hayes, E. "Insights from Women's Experiences for Teaching and Learning." In E. Hayes (ed.), *Effective Teaching Styles.* New Directions for Continuing Education, no. 43. San Francisco: Jossey-Bass, 1989.

Hayes, E., and Colin, S.A.J., III. *Racism and Sexism in the United States: Fundamental Issues.* New Directions for Adult and Continuing Education, no. 16. San Francisco: Jossey-Bass, 1994.

Hill-Collins, P. H. "The Social Construction of Black Feminist Thought." In M. Malson, E. Mudimbe-Boyi, J. O'Barr, and M. Wyer (eds.), *Black Women in America: Social Science Perspectives.* Chicago: University of Chicago Press, 1990.

Ihle, E. L. "Free Black Adult Education Before the Civil War." (Report No. RE I DEC 90). Boston: Paper presented at the Annual Meeting of the American Educational Research Association, 1990. (ED 321 099)

Johnstone, J.W.C., and Rivera, R. J. *Volunteers for Learning: A Study of the Educational Pursuits of Adults.* Hawthorne, N.Y.: Aldine, 1965.

Knowles, M. *The Modern Practice of Adult Education: From Pedagogy to Andragogy.* Englewood Cliffs, N.J.: Prentice Hall, 1980.

Knowles, M. *The Adult Leaner: A Neglected Species.* Houston: Gulf Publishing, 1984.

Kopka, T., and Peng, S. "Adult Education: Main Reasons for Participating. National Center for Education Statistics." (NCES Publication No. 93–451). Washington, D.C.: U.S. Department of Education. Office of Educational Research and Improvement, 1993.

Merriam, S. "Adult Learning: Where Have We Come From? Where Are We Headed?" New Directions for Adult and Continuing Education. San Francisco: Jossey-Bass, 1993.

Merriam, S., and Brockett, R. G. *The Profession and Practice of Adult Education: An Introduction.* San Francisco: Jossey-Bass, 1997.

National Center for Education Statistics. "Adult Literacy in America: A First Look at the Results of the National Adult Literacy Survey." (NCES Publication No. 065–000–00588–3) Washington, D.C.: U.S. Government Printing Office, 1994.

Quigley, B. A. "Hidden Logic: Reproduction and Resistance in Adult Literacy and Adult Basic Education." *Adult Education Quarterly,* 1990, *40*(2), 104–121.

Quigley, B. A. "Looking Back in Anger: The Influences of Schooling on Illiterate Adults." *Journal of Education,* 1992, *174.*

Scanlan, C., and Darkenwald, G. G. "Identifying Deterrents to Participation." *Adult Education Quarterly,* 1984, *34,* 155–166.

Sheared, V. "From Workfare to Edfare, African-American Women and the Elusive Quest for Self-Determination: A Critical Analysis of the JOBS Plan." University Microfilms International, 9230723, 1992.

Sheared, V. "Giving Voice: An Inclusive Model of Instruction—A Womanist Perspective." In E. Hayes and S.A.J. Colin III (eds.), *Confronting Racism and Sexism in Adult Education.* New Directions for Continuing Education, no. 61. San Francisco: Jossey-Bass, 1994a.

Sheared, V. "Participation of African American Adults in Traditional and Non-Traditional Adult Education Programs." Research report submitted to the California Department of Education, Adult Education Unit, Oct. 1994b.

Sheared, V. "The Significance of Including the Lived Experiences of African Americans in ABE Curriculum and Program Planning." 36th Annual Adult Education Research Conference Proceedings, 1995.

Sheared, V. "Giving Voice in an Adult Education Context." *College of Education Review*, San Francisco State University, 1996, 8.

Valentine, T., and James, R. "Education and African Americans: Implications of the 1990 Census for Adult Literacy Education." University of Georgia, Department of Adult Education, 1993.

VANESSA SHEARED is associate professor and chair of the Administration and Interdisciplinary Studies Department at San Francisco State University. She is also coordinator of the Adult Education Program.

4

Because human capital ideological assumptions drive most adult education programs serving Hispanics, the real social needs of Hispanics are overlooked in most adult education programs.

The Quest for Visibility in Adult Education: The Hispanic Experience

Jorge Jeria

The opportunity to write this chapter on Hispanics and adult education in the United States represents an attractive proposition and a challenge at the same time. It is attractive because it allows for the opening of cultural space in the field of adult education where little space has been available and for a discussion of the issues facing Hispanics in North American adult education. It is a challenge, however, because Hispanics have been stereotyped in a way that requires any writer to debunk the myths and inaccuracies that are commonly heard about the Hispanic population. We associate such stereotypical referents as *marginalized populations, immigrants,* and *second-language users* with Hispanics because these terms are widely used to characterize the Hispanic experience as one that is essentially alien to the experience other people in the United States have.

Another reason for the challenge is that Hispanics have been virtually invisible in the adult education research literature. Perhaps more disturbing is that despite their exclusion in research and scholarly works, Hispanics are well represented as "consumers" of adult education. A good indicator of this is the large number of books and materials for the market of second-language users and of general equivalence degree programs that cater to Hispanic learners. Another indicator is the large number of Hispanics who enroll in ESL (English as second language) programs, as well as other "deficit" programs, creating a good market for attracting needed dollars via grants to educational institutions.

This chapter presents an analysis of the participation of Hispanics in adult education. I first review the historical linkages between the United States and Latin America by way of providing a platform to discuss (1) how the migration of Hispanics throughout Latin America to the United States became intertwined with ESL education and (2) how that intertwining, in turn, is associated with human capital formation and the political economy of adult education. As a result, the cultural, linguistic, and national identity and heritage of Hispanics is threatened through apolitical, nonreflexive forms of adult education.

Hispanic American Diversity in the United States

Hispanic Americans represent a vastly diversified group of people whose common cultural origins are often overemphasized at the expense of the important differences that exist within this broad category of people. Hispanic Americans may include people called Mexican Americans, Chicanos, or Spanish Americans when they are born in North America; otherwise, the common denominator is the country of origin (Puerto Ricans, Cubans, Guatemalans, or Salvadorans) or the region they come from (Central or South Americans or Latin Americans) (U.S. Bureau of the Census, 1993a).

The designation *Hispanics* was used by the Bureau of the Census in the late 1970s to describe all persons in the United States who were descendants of people from Spanish-speaking or Portuguese-speaking (Brazil, for example) countries. A prime purpose was to simplify dealings with "the fastest-growing minority," which has the effect of eradicating particular histories and cultural heritage (Melville, 1989). Naming, of course, is not a neutral act. The term *Hispanic* does not denote ethnicity. The term *Hispanic American* is a complex word because its use is political rather than ethnic or cultural, but it is frequently used to denote a group of people with a common racial, ethnic, or cultural background. It has developed multiple meanings that suggest not only a political identity but also a social one. The term *Hispanic* is used to refer to individuals whose social origin is outside the United States but from a variety of Spanish-speaking countries, including Puerto Rico, Mexico, Cuba, and the Dominican Republic, in Central and South America. Therefore, it is important to understand that individuals who most North Americans commonly refer to as Hispanic or who are identified as Hispanic by the U.S. government actually employ other terms to identify themselves, including *Puerto Riqueños* and *Riqueñas*, *Chicanos* and *Chicanas*, and *Latinos* and *Latinas*. These words convey a sense of national or ethnic pride that extends beyond legal status. For example, the Chicano identity was forged out of the migrant worker struggle in the 1960s and 1970s for economic and social rights (Meier and Ribera, 1993).

To avoid the obvious linguistic awkwardness associated with trying to refer to the multiplicity of ethnicities, nationalities, and races that make up the Spanish-speaking population of the United States, I use the term *Hispanic* as a convenient and familiar word but with the understanding that it masks much of the diversity within that group. In addition, I use the term *immigrant* to refer to any person who participates in the social process of migration rather than to denote a person with a particular legal status. I believe that migration is a different, more fundamental right than the legal right that is associated with moving from country to country.

Demographic Profile of Hispanic Americans. Hispanic Americans are in fact the fastest-growing segment of the North American population. In 1990 Hispanic Americans made up approximately 9 percent of the U.S. population (U.S. Bureau of the Census, 1993a). Estimates are that in the year 2000, Hispanics will make up more than 11 percent of the population—about thirty-one million persons. This trend will continue so that by the year 2050, Hispanics will make up one-quarter of the population or nearly ninety-six million persons (U.S. Bureau of the Census, 1996).

In 1990 more than three-fifths of the total number of Hispanic Americans were Mexican in origin and resided predominantly in California and Texas. Puerto Ricans are the second-largest group and represent more than 12 percent of the total number of Hispanics. Puerto Ricans reside predominantly in New York, Florida, and Illinois. In fact, almost nine out of ten Hispanic Americans reside in ten states, with just over half of all Hispanic Americans living in California or Texas. Although most live in the Northeast and the Southwest, there is great dispersion among Hispanic Americans throughout the United States (U.S. Bureau of the Census, 1993a).

Socioeconomic Factors. Socioeconomic factors affect this population in important ways. For example, in 1992 the poverty rate among all Hispanics was 29 percent, compared with the national average of 11 percent. However, this figure varied significantly within the Hispanic population. The poverty rate for Mexican Americans was 30 percent, for Puerto Ricans 36.5 percent, and for Cubans 18.1 percent. In 1993 just over half of Hispanics (53.1 percent) had completed high school, whereas only 9 percent had completed college. The national averages were 81 percent and 21 percent, respectively (U.S. Bureau of the Census, 1993a).

However, despite some progress Hispanic Americans continued to lag behind in education and income status. For example, in 1993 median family income was $23,714 for Mexican Americans, $20,301 for Puerto Ricans, and $31,015 for Cuban Americans. In addition, the Mexican American population is becoming increasingly urbanized, with more than four in ten living in metropolitan areas (Bean and Tienda, 1987). Increased educational opportunities and tightly knit communities have led to the development of a new middle class. However, many well-to-do Hispanics leave the "barrio" (lower-working-class communities). One of the cultural consequences of this development is that fewer Hispanic children have cultural knowledge about their language and history (Acuña, 1988).

Culture and Ethnicity Among Hispanics. Hispanics trace their racial and ethnic heritage to three primary origins: Spanish, African, and Native American. Historically, Spanish kingdoms had long maintained contact with Africans of the North. Three centuries of Moorish invasion left strong marks in the culture of the Iberian peninsula. However, because race was constructed differently, the biological and cultural heritage of many Hispanics is intermixed. By 1900 the African identity among Hispanics was so intermixed that there was no separate African identity, especially within Mexican American areas (Franklin and Moss, 1994). For example, the biological heritage of most Mexican *mestizos* is more Indian than Spanish or African, and for Puerto Ricans the primary identity is cultural rather than racial (Rodriguez, 1991).

According to Carlson (1990), the "first Europeans to settle permanently in the United States were from Spain and not from England in 1598 in the Upper Rio Grande Valley" (cited in Haverluk, 1996, p. 134). Therefore, the experience of other minorities within the context of Anglo-American colonization and later nationalization of the North American continent can be juxtaposed against that of the Spanish which, in many areas of North America, predates that of the English. Even though all historical claims to land must be seen in light of those of the Native Americans who predated European occupation, the history of Hispanic Americans can be seen as one in which the expansion of the Anglo-American presence was at the expense of native and Spanish-speaking peoples. It is the experience of colonialism and discrimination that underscores the experience of Hispanic Americans in the United States and provides a common basis from which to create an Hispanic identity.

Historical Highlights on Hispanics in the United States

For a better understanding of these conditions, it is important to provide a historical perspective on Hispanics in the United States, which will include a discussion of the relation of the United States to Latin America, migration issues such as population trends and changes, the socioeconomic patterns of Hispanics in the United States, and language issues.

Beginning with Mexico alone, we find a variety of indigenous cultures and languages from northern to southern Mexico, as well as regional differences from the Atlantic coast to the Pacific coast. We also find these differences in Central America, South America, and the Andean region. Spanish in some of these areas is only a second language, whereas indigenous languages such as Nahual, Aymara, and Quechua or Amazonic dialects are first languages. Much of the Atlantic coast of Latin America (in particular, Brazil), and in many cases the Pacific coast, was permeated by the results of slavery, that is, there were large African populations. Colonialism had a strong influence in Latin America from Spanish, Portuguese, English, and French to Dutch colonizers because Latin America was the ground for expansive European capitalism in silver mining and slave trading, and in developing sugar cane plantations. Later, European migration provided new waves of settlers as part of a mass population movement.

The relationship between the United States and Latin America is longstanding. It has included overt U.S. military action in the Mexican War in 1845, the Spanish-American War in 1898, and an intervention in Panama in 1989. It has also included foreign policy initiatives such as President Theodore Roosevelt's "backyard policy" at the turn of the twentieth century. Furthermore, it has included covert military action in Guatemala, El Salvador, Cuba, and Chile from the 1960s to the 1990s.

Currently, issues relating to drug certification, border patrol, and immigrants' rights indicate that relationships even in recent times with the rest of the Latin American continent have always been strained. In this context, the historical relationship of the United States with Mexico, Puerto Rico, and Cuba is part of the colonial territorial and economic expansion by Spain first and the United States later. Because the United States has lost much of its dominant position in the hemisphere and the cold war is no longer a basis for military interventions in Latin American politics, economic regionalization may lead to a more equitable relationship between the United States and the Latin American countries.

Nativistic Sentiments and Hispanic Immigration. Nativism has been a recurrent theme in U.S. policy toward non-European immigrants. The passage of the 1986 Immigration Control and Reform Act (ICRA) marked a high point of anti-Hispanic sentiment in the United States. This was most evident in the English Only movement of the 1980s and the early 1990s, when a number of states and municipalities approved referenda to make English the "official" language. Although the legal implications of such acts were ambiguous, it is clear that strong anti-Hispanic sentiments fueled the movement. For example, California continues to be the center of many nativistic activities, due mainly to its high concentration of Hispanics and other non-European immigrants. In 1994, Proposition 187 was a major issue in the California governor's election. Then governor Pete Wilson clearly campaigned on the issue and supported legislation to restrict the rights of so-called illegals in accessing welfare, workers' benefits, and educational benefits, including bilingual education. Despite such efforts, the Hispanic population continues to grow and will continue to have an impact on the provision of education to non-English speaking populations.

Such movements as the English Only movement serve to underscore the way English language literacy is driven by labor market needs, as defined by politicians, business leaders, and educators. Literacy in industrialized countries is viewed as an index of talent, skill, and intelligence. Adults who do not possess English language fluency are considered to be less able and less useful in the American labor market. The fact of the matter is that Hispanics account for an overrepresentation of workers in occupations requiring manual labor, such as in the agricultural industry. Educators who operate under the assumption that strong written and verbal skills are sure signs of education and social mobility view migrant workers as ignorant and unskilled. In this context the analysis of Bourdieu and Passeron (1977) is important in terms of how society assigns value to education and devalues those whose cultural capital is regarded as a deficit. Clearly, acquiring the language is promoted as an "acquisition of cultural

capital" that can be exchanged in the market for goods and services. This perspective, coupled with the social and historical distortions regarding the experience of Hispanic Americans, contributes to the absence of a significant Hispanic presence in the education literature.

Hispanic Americans as Human Capital. *Human capital* refers to characteristics and capabilities possessed by individuals who enhance economic productivity. Bourdieu explains cultural capital as "the structure of the distribution of instruments for the appropriation of symbolic wealth socially designated as worthy of being sought and processed" (Bourdieu, 1977, p. 488). In the context of adult education for Hispanics, language becomes a cultural commodity that, once learned, can be exchanged for socially valued material goods. Closely related to the concept of human capital is *social capital*, which can be defined as "tools and training that enhance individual productivity" (Putnam, 1995, p. 67). Both concepts deem individuals or collectivities as resources for capital and economic development. Whereas *human capital* refers to individual assets, *social capital* is a property of human collectivities.

The concept of human and cultural capital is useful in understanding the attitude of Anglo-Americans toward Hispanic Americans. Although many Anglo-Americans have harbored prejudice toward Hispanics, there have been times when Hispanics, especially Mexicans, have been welcomed to the United States. The Bracero program during the 1940s is a case in point. During World War II, the shortage of labor in many agricultural industries led planters and growers to appeal to the U.S. government to permit Mexicans to enter the United States for the purpose of providing needed labor. The U.S. and Mexican governments established the Bracero program, which allowed Mexican workers to enter the United States during the growing season. However, these workers had to return to Mexico when the growing season was over. The influx of Mexicans during the 1940s and early 1950s fueled fears among whites living in states adjacent to Mexico. The program was effectively ended when the Wetback program repatriated almost all Mexicans who had arrived in the United States under the Bracero program (McWilliams, 1968).

It can be concluded on the basis of these examples that, to the degree that Hispanics are viewed as useful resources for economic productivity, they have been welcomed into the United States. To the degree that they have been seen as an economic drain, Hispanics have been unwelcome. The economic exploitation of Hispanics has shaped a good deal of educational practice toward Hispanics as a group as well.

Hispanic Migration. Hispanic immigrants have entered the United States with a different socioeconomic status than other immigrant groups such as (Asian) Indians, Taiwanese, or Nigerians. Latin Americans "have high rates of labor force participation but well below-average levels of educational attainment and they are concentrated in lower-collar employment" (Rumbaut, 1995). However, the breakdown by national origin indicates that there are differences among countries. South Americans from Venezuela, Argentina, Bolivia, and Chile show higher economic status and higher educational level when compared with other Latin American immigrants, "suggesting that these groups consist substantially of highly-skilled persons who have entered under the occupational preferences of U.S. immigration laws" (Rumbaut, 1995).

Economic Factors. Historically, economic pressures have been a major factor contributing to the migration of Hispanics. Since 1830, the westward expansion of the United States economy has provided the basis for a continuous Mexican migration. Hispanics have served as migrant workers in Wyoming, Nebraska, and Colorado; they have worked in the "irrigated valleys" of the West, the sugar beet plantation regions of the North and South Platte Rivers, and the vegetable-growing areas of California (Haverluk, 1996). From 1942 to 1964, the Bracero program expanded Mexican migration to areas such Yakima, Washington, Idaho, and Texas (Haverluk, 1996). Another impact of this migration was the growth in the Mexican population in the Midwest, mainly Chicago, and the industrial belt of the Gary-Chicago area.

American Imperialism. Other factors that contributed to the pattern of migration were American colonialism, territorial expansion, and the economic and ideological hegemony of the United States throughout Latin America. The acquisition of Puerto Rico following the Spanish-American War in 1898 established an incentive for Puerto Ricans to migrate to the United States in ways that affected the large cities of the eastern part of the United States, particularly New York. The reaction of the U.S. government to the Castro takeover of Cuba led to the influx of Cubans during the late 1950s and early 1960s to South Florida. And a large number of people from Central America entered the United States in recent years due to the wars in El Salvador and Guatemala, as well as the destabilization program promoted by U.S. foreign policy in Nicaragua. An important conclusion to draw from this historical perspective is that Hispanics have resided in or migrated to the United States for decades. The popular view of Hispanics as recent immigrants is incorrect.

Attempts to change the government's policy toward the migration of Hispanics to the United States have led to restrictions on immigration and greater controls placed on the identification of "illegal" aliens in the United States. As a result of changes in the restrictive National Origins Act of 1924 and later the Immigration and Nationality Act of 1965, the U.S. Bureau of the Census differentiated Puerto Ricans, Cubans, and Mexicans from Central Americans. The 1965 act allowed for family reunification, which increased the number of immigrants, mainly from Asia and Latin America. These groups settled in urban areas and closer to main cities in the southwest and eastern parts of the United States. During the 1980s Salvadorans, Dominicans, Jamaicans, Guatemalans, and Colombians entered the United States in large numbers, followed by Peruvians and Ecuadoreans. The main increase however was "registered from Guyanese immigrants making them the fastest-growing immigrant group from South America" (Rumbaut, 1995, p. 12).

The Politics of Language Diversity

With the growing concentration of Hispanics in parts of the United States, the debate over language and its role in U.S. business and politics has increased in importance. Attempts at the enforcement of a monolingual policy, in practice if not in policy, has been an important means to blurring cultural, social, and economic differences in the United States. The English Only movement in the 1980s and early 1990s in various states and municipalities became an ideological weapon to reduce the impact of large concentrations of Hispanics throughout the nation. A 1993 *Chicago Tribune* headline read: "Citizenship Ceremony In Spanish Enrages English-Only Advocates." In this story, English Only advocates objected to Hispanic immigrants taking the oath of citizenship in Spanish rather than English. Stories like this appear from time to time, displaying the resiliency of English Only forces. The sentiment that seems most reflective of this movement is "if all these people are going to come here, the least they can do is learn our language" (p. 3).

A monolingual policy has also been a way to suppress different histories of the United States. Challenging the supposed linguistic and cultural unity of the United States gives rise to the idea of society with multiple histories. Additionally, a linguistic homogeneity homogenizes all Hispanic Americans into a single group—non-English speakers. Linguistic diversity challenges this homogenization and its accompanying idea of a monocultural society.

The politics of language becomes even more prominent when examining the future in terms of the growth of the numbers of Hispanics. The increasing numbers of immigrants speaking a language other than English will continue to rise (Perez and de la Rosa Salazar, 1993; McManus, William, and Finus, 1983; Stolzenberg and Tienda, 1997). Census bureau data indicate that by 1990, one in seven U.S. residents would not speak a language other than English at home. Furthermore, 6.7 million Americans would not speak English well or at all (U.S. Bureau of the Census, 1993a). By the year 2000, more than twenty million U.S. residents will speak a language other than English as their first language (Veltman, 1990; Stolzenberg and Tienda, 1997). The majority of these people are from Asia and Latin America. The increasing numbers of Americans for whom English is not their first language will certainly increase the pressure against the English Only movement and raise the issue of language diversity, not only in primary and adult education but also in the workplace. It might be anticipated that the opponents of language diversity will redouble their efforts to enforce a monolingual policy in areas where there are high concentrations of non-English speakers.

Linguistic Diversity and Economic Productivity

Language difference is also an economic issue. Given that economic reasons are the driving force behind Hispanic migration, labor market access in the United States becomes a fundamental issue for Hispanic adults. English language learning, therefore, has become the necessary element in labor market success for Hispanics.

Consequently, low educational attainment coupled with discrimination is a major factor limiting job access. Because many Hispanic Americans are in migrant, agricultural jobs or low-paying manual labor jobs, this problem becomes nearly insoluble; these workers do not have the skills to move into higher-paying positions and cannot get access to quality educational and social services because they are poor. For adult educators working with these populations, it is not enough to simply teach English language skills. English proficiency in and of itself will not address the problem of discrimination that workers face in the workplace. Language learning, coupled with problem solving and political and social action, may begin to provide a way to address the problems Hispanic adults face.

Language learning also intersects with the issue of welfare reform. In the discussion on welfare reform, language has been used to deny access to social services to immigrants who do not speak English. Thus, we find that a large percentage of Hispanic adults learn English because language fluency is equated with preparation to enter the workforce or ability to access social services. The implication of this is that ESL instructors have to address not only English language skills but also job-related and social service issues.

It is important to note that language needs to be considered along with other elements such as schooling and ethnic discrimination in order to obtain a clear picture of this issue. As stated earlier, Hispanics as a whole have a low educational attainment due, in part, to the steady flow of Mexican immigrants. Because Mexicans dominate the Hispanic category it affects the aggregated statistics as well (Aponte, 1996). This suggests that low educational attainment may not necessarily be a trend for Hispanics, especially second- and third-generation Hispanics. Low educational attainment is more evident in areas of higher reception of immigrants such as Chicago, Los Angeles, Miami, and New York.

It is also known that many Hispanic immigrants with little schooling also have little fluency in English; they have entered employment mainly in the informal sector of the economy. Also, many immigrants tend to be young adults searching for employment, typically in seasonal or migrant agricultural work. We also find areas reshaped by the economy by virtue of economic globalization. Such is the case in the meatpacking industry and in service areas such as hotels and restaurants that are characterized by nonunionization and part-time employment. This type of labor market is clearly segmented; there are no possibilities of climbing the merit ladder. This, united with cultural barriers and lack of interpersonal networks accessible only to the most educated groups in society, allows for a very limited employability. This would suggest that a viable solution is not necessarily acquiring language skills only but acquiring schooling. Thus, language becomes only a medium and not an end in itself. Learning the language may not necessarily, under this circumstance, provide the possibility of participating in a wider employment pool but participating only in "dedicated employment pockets" or language enclaves that operate in employment markets where it is acceptable to have little or no skill in speaking English.

Today, social and economic changes have "generated a flurry of new jobs for the old Hispanic American population which today is needed to perform a new array of culturally appropriate and language specific tasks in the various social and private agencies" (Gouveia, 1997, p. 11). Thus, a much clearer picture emerges between adult education and this population. This relationship has taken place specifically in the area of language training in order to participate in employment pools and skills training of a diverse nature to perform jobs. Due to the nature of Hispanic employment, language skills represent only one aspect of the total picture. Other factors that influence and affect the economic position of Hispanics have been associated with discrimination and a low quality of education.

Hispanics Absent from Adult Education Literature

There is relatively little research about Hispanics as adult learners in the field of adult education. The few studies that have been reported have employed a deficit perspective to interpret the Hispanic experience in adult education. The description of the educational experience of Hispanics is generally viewed as needing remedial language in order to assimilate culturally to U.S. society (Diaz-Lefebre, 1990; Facundo, 1984; Heany, 1989; Howlett, 1998; Jeria, 1990, 1992; Young and Padilla, 1990). Such outsider conceptual frameworks only perpetuate the damage done to learners in alien educational settings.

Furthermore, Hispanic adult education is discussed as an instance of "minority education" in order to indicate the marginalized status of Hispanic Americans. This approach highlights the fact that Hispanics are frequently viewed as aliens who have come from another country and who do not fit neatly into U.S. society. Hispanics do not share equitably in the political, wealth, and material benefits of the United States. As a consequence, adult education for Hispanic Americans is most often associated with adult second-language training (Guglielmino, 1991). Thus, what is offered as education to the Hispanic population is training in a language in which they are asked to reproduce cultural symbols that teachers of adults think they don't have—in other words, they are working from a deficit.

The consequence of viewing Hispanics in adult education from a deficit and minority perspective is to make Hispanics invisible to the field of adult education. By this I want to argue that mainstream adult educators do not incorporate Hispanic sociocultural factors and historical issues that define the experience of Hispanics in America in developing programs that serve Hispanic American learners. Rather, adult educators tend to employ top-down, authoritarian, assimilationist models of education. In effect, this approach renders the Hispanic experience invisible to the practice and research in adult education.

Top-down models typically employ a competency-based approach to language learning, ignore significant linguistic differences that exist among various Spanish-speaking groups, and are geared toward socializing non-native speakers into American linguistic and sociocultural conventions. For example, a report on the evaluation of services of the Job Training and Partnership Act (JTPA) programs suggests that new models of serving Hispanics be developed that address the linguistic and cultural differences among Hispanics as a step toward improving services and increasing the number of Hispanics who would enroll in JTPA programs. "Continued use" educational models based on cultural assimilation in language training points to the dominance of the English language as the norm in American society. The effect of such models of education is to limit adult education services to Hispanic Americans (National Commission for Employment Policy, 1990).

Community-Based and Popular Education Programs

Although assimilation and bilingual education are commonplace, popular education is an approach to education that has strong roots in the Hispanic community, both in the United States and in Latin American countries. Because popular education is itself a marginalized form of adult education, the strong Hispanic influence on its development as a means to meeting community needs is often overlooked. Community-based adult education programs simply do not attract the interest, resources, or attention of adult education practitioners or scholars (Merriam and Brockett, 1997).

Community-based adult education programs like popular education have been considered as "alternative" to adult education programs sponsored by the state. The essence of popular education can be summarized by saying that popular education is considered a modality of adult education for the people with the objective of developing an education created by the people. Cantera, a popular education agency located in Managua, Nicaragua, defines *popular education* as "a holistic, integrated form of education that is at once born from and responsible for the raising of people's consciousness of the strength of their communities in action. It is called popular because it comes from the populace, out of the needs and experience of the people themselves" (Cantera, 1998).

Popular education programs are aimed at helping community members address specific problems. They help learners articulate the political relationship between theoretical knowledge and the knowledge they already possess about their daily experience and practice. In this process, the creation of knowledge through a pedagogical articulation of informal and formal knowledge is essential. Popular education proposes a renewed relationship between man, society, and culture. In other words, education leads in the quest for liberatory action by focusing on democratic participation of learners, praxis, and social change.

Essentially, popular education is political. Its primary aim is to facilitate the development of projects or movements that focus the interests of one class of people against those of a privileged class. Ultimately, the objective of popular education is to produce change that strikes at the heart of capitalist hegemony. This is accomplished by adopting a critical pedagogical strategy that decenters power and authority from traditional institutional structures and processes to local, community-based forms (Stanage, 1995).

On a community level, popular education focuses on the needs and culture of communities and involves reflection on relevant aspects of learners' lives. The process aims to help learners use their daily life and experiences as reference points for evaluating the knowledge they produce (Freire, 1994). Popular education "works to make space for the collective production of knowledge and insight, and builds on what emerges from the experiences of those actively participating" (Walters and Manicom, 1997, p. 2). Thus, popular education aims to help learners see their own experience as a valuable resource for examining problems they face in their communities. In this regard, nonformal and informal learning become important processes of knowledge creation so that learners can develop their own theory about work, culture, and citizenship.

The Importance of Popular and Community Education. Based on the foregoing, one could surmise that support for popular education as a model of adult education for serving Hispanic Americans is widely accepted. The influence of the writings and the organizing of Paulo Freire and the popular adult education movement that has flourished in Latin American countries since the 1970s had a significant impact on adult education within the Hispanic community (Heany, 1989). Ideas about popular education, as well as organizations that support popular education, have increased as the number of immigrants from Latin America arrive who are influenced by Freirian education (Gonzalez, 1994).

For example, the Universidad Popular (Chicago) and the Institute for Popular Education (New York City), to name two examples, are community-based organizations that serve Hispanic immigrants in their communities through political action and popular education. However, there is little description or analysis of the ways in which popular adult education programs such as these effect change in these communities. And what little analysis exists is not easily accessible by practitioners seeking to improve the way educational services are provided in Hispanic communities.

If popular education programs are considered to be educational sites where issues of daily survival, migration, and other problems that Hispanic immigrants face when entering a new culture (Heany, 1989) are adequately addressed, then it is easy to see how the absence of an Hispanic presence in the adult education literature would occur. The limited scope of the literature is important to observe here because new forms of reconceptualizing adult education become pointers to social problems.

Consequently, unless popular education becomes more than an alternative to the traditional forms of adult education that serve Hispanic Americans, the need will continue for a more consistent dialogue between policymakers and popular educators. The challenge for adult educators is to break the cycle of stereotypes and establish wider referents when discussing this population.

The point for discussion here is to open areas usually not considered in adult education such as the historical and political links of Latin America and the United States and the resulting foreign policy and its links to immigrants' movements. From these perspectives adult educators can gain an understanding about Hispanics and adult education's connection to sociopolitical and cultural issues, as well as issues of power, ideology, and human capital formation.

Adult Education as Export. Following the Cuban Revolution of 1959, the U.S. cold war policy toward Latin America was punctuated by military interventions that were supplemented by economic and social development programs. One of these programs, The Alliance for Progress, was the response by the United States to counter the increasing unrest and possible "communist takeover" of Latin American countries. This program brought to Latin America, among other products, adult education under the "brand" of "andragogy" (Jeria, 1997) and literacy projects in Recife, Brazil (Jeria, 1989). Thus, a historical analysis provides an explanation of the earlier statement that Hispanics are neither newcomers nor recent immigrants and that their invisibility in this field is probably a product of historical neglect resulting from earlier policies toward Latin America. Thus, the relationship between the United States and Latin America has been twofold. On one side, American foreign policy to Latin American countries was mediated by U.S. concerns about a communist presence in Latin America that led to a rapprochement between the United States and Latin America. On the other, continued patterns of migration from Latin American countries to the United States led to a growing nativism that viewed Hispanics with a sense of skepticism and prejudice.

Adult education has not served as an agent for Hispanic revitalization in the United States. Driven by human capital assumptions about the need for labor and overlaid with nativistic and assimilationist sentiment, adult education has provided a means to subsistence living in the United States for Hispanics. In order to combat the ethnocentric and exclusionist consequences of adult education for Hispanics, adult educators should consider the following in developing programs for Hispanic learners:

Learn about and understand the social, political, and economic history of Hispanics, especially of the particular ethnic or national group being served. The history of Puerto Ricans is very different than the history of Chicanos.

Language learning is only one priority for Spanish-speaking learners. Cultural adjustment, as well as political awareness and action, are key factors that adult educators should address in adult education programs for Hispanics.

Adult educators should model educational practice and procedures based on popular education models that have strong roots in Hispanic communities.

Resources available for adult educators can be accessed both on-line and through community organization networks in cities where there are large Hispanic populations, like Los Angeles, Chicago, Miami, and New York.

Hispanic culture and language should serve as resources for instruction rather than seen as marginal to the demands of living in the predominantly English-speaking country. Hispanic literature, theater, music, and customs should be incorporated into learning activities.

Factors Affecting Hispanic Adult Education

A number of factors shape the relationship between adult education and the Hispanic population. Despite the basic educational needs related to cultural estrangement associated with movement from one language context to another, Hispanics will continue to be consumers of adult education and will remain invisible in the field of adult education for some time to come. The culture of adult education in its present state does not acknowledge the needs of Hispanics as a group with its own sociocultural and political needs. Most often, Hispanics are considered immigrants pursuing some work-related training for insertion in the U.S. labor market. Little research exists concerning their status as members of a particular culture served by the system of adult education.

Adult education, premised on human capital perspectives of work, labor market needs, and acculturation, divests Hispanics of any sense of educational ownership and self-determination. Most often, language learning and job training are reduced to mere skill acquisition, thus reproducing social inequities that already plague Hispanic Americans. Moreover, when using the concepts of cultural capital and human capital formation, and associating them to historical neglect embodied in policies to Latin America, we find that anyone under the stamp of "Hispanic" will be placed in a category of "deficit." Perhaps more incongruent is the fact that a collective name "Hispanic" is applied to individuals, thus transferring those deficit regardless of their individuality.

Given the wider scope of adult education activity, more and more Hispanics will be served by adult education; thus, the issues associated with the United States' fast-growing minority will become even more prominent. Adult educators must recognize and understand the complexities of this group from a historical perspective of U.S. relations with Latin America. The following are issues that adult education, as a field, must address in order to improve services to Hispanics.

Educational Attainment. Adult educators need to consider how low educational attainment affects the adult education needs of Hispanics. Basic language and literacy skills provide a minimum threshold for adult education program planning. It is known that for many Hispanic adults the completion of high school is not sufficient for employment. For others it may not even guarantee adequate literacy and numeracy skills. Adult educators frequently lack resources to provide students with a competitive education. However, as with other citizens and residents in the United States, Hispanics need to know how to interact effectively with employers, social service agencies, and the government to ensure that their rights are protected. This kind of knowledge should be important, regardless of language proficiency or educational level and therefore should be a part of all activist-oriented educational programming for Hispanic adults.

Discrimination in the Workplace. Hispanics are susceptible to workplace discrimination because they frequently are not aware of their rights and because they fear government identification due to the political stance of federal agencies like the Immigration Naturalization Service (INS). The INS history of acting in a punitive way toward Hispanics creates a climate of distrust that allows discrimination to go unchecked in the workplace. Despite the activism of migrant workers in the 1960s and 1970s, much work remains to be done to ensure workers' rights. Adult educators must address these issues in adult education programs to ensure that learners are not forced to go "underground" to preserve their economic security. This is especially true of those with limited English proficiency who are easily targeted as illegals (Perez and de la Rosa Salazar, 1993).

Relating the Formal to Nonformal Education. Adult educators should search out resources and strategies to make adult education less like standard schooling and more like informal community-based education. Although many providers of adult education services to Hispanics are public bureaucracies, institutional obstacles that inhibit programmatic cultural change at the interior of the adult education process must be overcome. Formal institutional testing, requests for Social Security numbers, identification of family members, and other procedures create resistance among potential participants. Balance needs to be found between legitimate institutional documentation and reporting requirements and the basic educational needs of the Hispanics who are served by those programs.

Shared Participation in Educational Programming. Participation in adult education should be understood here not as "enrolled to receive instruction" but as being part of the decision-making process, creating cultural spaces in curricular issues, and going beyond the formal requirements of training to more complex issues of daily life within the Hispanic community. Finally, adult education should look beyond human capital formation when dealing with Hispanics, thus considering them as subjects with cultural and different experiences and not as objects able to perform in the labor market.

Conclusion

Hispanic Americans will become the largest ethnic minority group in the United States in the twenty-first century. In order to serve this growing population more effectively, adult education programs, adult educators, and education policy makers must acknowledge the political, cultural, and language issues that impact the lives of Hispanics in the United States. Failure to do so will continue to leave Hispanic Americans marginalized and invisible within the adult education discourse. Resources such as popular education programs serve as models for how to improve services to Hispanics.

References

Acuña, R. *Occupied America: A History of Chicanos.* (3rd ed.) New York: Harper & Row, 1988.

Aponte, R. *NAFTA and Mexican Migration to Michigan and the U.S.* Julian Samora Research Institute. Working paper no. 25, Mar. 1996.

Bean, F. D., and Tienda, M. *The Hispanic Population of the United States.* New York: Russell Sage Foundation, 1987.

Bourdieu, P. "Cultural Reproduction and Social Reproduction." In J. Karabel and A. H. Halsey. *Power and Ideology in Education.* New York: Oxford University Press, 1977.

Bourdieu, P., and Passeron, J-C. *Reproduction in Education, Society, and Culture.* London: Sage Publications, 1977.

Cantera Popular Education and Communication Center. *Cantera's Approach to Popular Education.* Available on-line: http:\\www.oneworld.org\cantera\education\index.html, 1998.

Chicago *Tribune.* "Those English only demands speak mostly of prejudice." *Chicago Tribune,* Sept. 28, 1993.

Diaz-Lefebre, R. "The Hispanic Adult Learner in a Rural Community College." In B. Cassara (ed.), *Adult Education in a Multicultural Society.* London, New York: Routledge, 1990.

Facundo, B. "Issues for an Evaluation of Freire-Inspired Programs in the United States and Puerto Rico." Report for the Latino Institute, 1984.

Franklin, J. H., and Moss, A. A., Jr. *From Slavery to Freedom: A History of Negro Americans.* (7th ed.) New York: Knopf, 1994.

Freire, P. *Pedagogy of Hope: Reliving Pedagogy of the Oppressed.* New York: Continuum, 1994.

Gonzalez, M. "The Voice of Latinas." *Harvard Educational Review,* 1994, 6 (4), 33–45.

Gouveia, L. "Welfare Reform: A New Nativism Neglects the Facts." *Nexo,* Winter 1977, (2), 8–9, 11, 16.

Guglielmino, L. M. (ed.). *Adult ESL Instruction: Sourcebook.* Glenview, Ill.: Scott, Foresman, 1991.

Haverluk, T. "The Changing Geography of U.S. Hispanics, 1850–1990." *Journal of Geography,* (May-June), 1996.

Heany, T. *Struggling to Be Free.* DeKalb, Ill.: Lindeman Center, Northern Illinois University, 1989.

Howlett, L. "A Field Study of Hispanic Ecclesial Based Communities in Northern Illinois: The Promise or Compromise of Popular Education." Unpublished doctoral dissertation, Northern Illinois University, DeKalb, 1998.

Jeria, J. "Adult Education in Latin America." *Thresholds,* 1989, *XV* (4), 39–42.

Jeria, J. "Popular Education: Models that Contribute to the Empowerment of Learners in Minority Communities." In J. Ross-Gordon, and others (eds.), *Serving Culturally Diverse Populations.* New Directions in Adult Continuing Education, no. 48. San Francisco: Jossey-Bass, 1990.

Jeria, J. "Hispanic Community Development in the United States: Its Social Economic and Cultural Aspects." Paper presented at the International Society for Intercultural Education, Training and Research (SIETAR), Kingston, Jamaica, 1992.

Jeria, J. "NAFTA and the Political Economy of Adult Education." Paper presented at the 9th World Congress of Comparative Education Societies, Sydney, Australia, 1997.

Meier, M. S., and Ribera, F. *Mexican Americans/American Mexicans: From Conquistadors to Chicanos.* New York: Hill & Wang, 1993.

Melville, M. "Hispanics: Race Class to Ethnicity?" *Journal of Ethnic Studies,* 1989, *16* (1), 69–83.

Merriam, S., and Brockett, R. *The Profession and Practice of Adult Education.* San Francisco: Jossey-Bass, 1997.

McManus, W., William, G., and Finus, W. "Earning of Hispanic Men: The Role of English Language Proficiency." *Journal of Labor Economics,* 1983, *1,* 101–130.

McWilliams, C. *Northward from Mexico. The Spanish Speaking People of the United States.* New York: Greenwood Press, 1968.

National Commission for Employment Policy. "Training Hispanics: Implications for the JTPA System. Special Report Number 27." Washington, D.C.: U.S. Department of Labor, 1990.

Perez, S., and de la Rosa Salazar, D. "Economic, Labor Force and Social Implications of Latino Educational and Population Trends." *Hispanic Journal of Behavioral Sciences, 15* (2), 1993, 188–229.

Putnam, R. "Bowling Alone: American's Declining Social Capital." *Journal of Democracy,* 1995, *6,* 65–78.

Rodriguez, C. E. *Puerto Ricans Born in the United States.* Boulder, Colo.: Westview, 1991.

Rumbaut, G. R. "Immigrants from Latin America and the Caribbean: A Socioeconomic Profile." *CIFRAS* No.6, the Julian Samora Research Institute, Michigan State University, 1995.

Stanage, S. M. "Popular Education as Adult Education within Postmodernism." *Thresholds in Education,* 1995, *22,* 3–4.

Stolzenberg, R. M., and Tienda, M. "English Proficiency, Education and the Conditional Economic Assimilation of Hispanics and Asian Origin Men." *Social Science Research,* 1997, *26,* 25–51.

U.S. Bureau of the Census. *We, the Hispanic Americans.* Washington, D.C.: U.S. Government Printing Office. 1993a.

U.S. Bureau of the Census. "Hispanic Americans Today." *Current Population Reports, Population Characteristics.* Washington, D.C.: U.S. Government Printing Office, 1993b.

U.S. Bureau of the Census. *Resident Population of the United States: Middle Series Projections, 1996–2000, by Sex, Race, and Hispanic Origin, with Median Age Source.* Washington, D.C.: U.S. Government Printing Office, 1996.

Veltman, C. "The Status of the Spanish Language in the United States at the Beginning of the 21st Century." *International Migration Review,* 1990, *24* (1), 108–123.

Walters, S., and Manicom, L. (eds.). *Gender in Popular Education: Methods for Empowerment,* London: Zed Books, 1997.

Young, E., and Padilla, M. "Mujeres Unidas en Accion: A Popular Education Process." *Harvard Educational Review,* 1990, *60* (1), 1–18.

JORGE JERIA is associate professor of adult education in the Department of Leadership and Educational Policy Studies at Northern Illinois University, DeKalb.

5

Examples of culturally relevant education programs for Navajo adults are discussed in terms of program particulars and participants.

Navajo Language and Culture in Adult Education

Louise Lockard

This chapter focuses on native language literacy for Navajo adults in four settings: a state prison, a tribal community college, an urban community center, and a family literacy project. A profile of each program shows the struggle of adult Navajo learners to reclaim voice and to move into the future in each setting. Henry Giroux (1987) writes that to be literate is "to be present and active in the struggle for reclaiming one's voice, history, and future" (p. 11). Alvin Tsingine, a Navajo inmate at the Arizona State Prison, echoes Giroux's concept of critical literacy when he writes,

> I personally cannot speak fluent Navajo and do not read or write the language either. The other Navajos that I have talked with here are many like myself. Maintaining our cultural and traditional identity is very important to us and regaining the spirituality of our ancestors. One way of doing this is to learn to speak, read and write in our own native language [letter to the author May 4, 1997].

In each of the adult education settings reviewed in the sections to follow, language learning is central to the development of cultural identity, which, in turn, is an important aspect of being Navajo in the modern world.

The Context of Place

The Navajo Nation, which is located in the four-corners region of the states of Arizona, Utah, New Mexico, and Colorado, has a population of more than 165,000. The Treaty of 1868 with the United States government established the sovereignty of the Navajo Nation. Today, the Navajo Nation is governed by an elected president and tribal council, which consists of eighty-eight elected community representatives. Eleven council members serve on the Navajo Nation education committee, which advises the Division of Diné Education—the tribal education department that functions at the level of a state education agency for federal grants. Navajo students are educated in U.S. Bureau of Indian Affairs boarding and day schools, contact and grant schools, public schools, and schools chartered by the state of Arizona.

Most families on the Navajo Nation live below the federal poverty level. For example, in 1997 the average per capita income of Navajo families was estimated to be $4,106. More than half (57.4 percent) of all families live below the federal poverty level. Furthermore, almost three of ten persons aged sixteen or older (29.7 percent) are unemployed (Division of Diné Education, 1997). Poverty and joblessness affect the ability of the average Navajo family to provide adequate housing for their children. Half of all housing units on the Navajo Nation lack complete plumbing and kitchen facilities. One-third of all houses do not have running water. Over half of all houses lack sewer or septic tank systems, and 77.5 percent lack telephones (Division of Diné Education, 1997).

It is a paradox of American Indian cultures that native languages are not being transmitted between the older and younger generations. Of 155 American Indian languages, 87 percent are spoken by adults who no longer teach them to their children. Many languages will no longer be spoken within a generation. More than one-third of American Indian and Alaskan Native languages have fewer than one hundred speakers. Today, Navajos constitute 45 percent of all speakers of American Indian languages.

The Historical Context

The history of Navajo-United States relations is marked by American exploitation and Navajo struggle to maintain a distinct nation. In 1868, the Navajos signed a treaty with the federal government allowing them to return from Ft. Sumner, New Mexico, to portions of their former territory in Arizona and eastern New Mexico—a distance of more than five hundred miles. The treaty also allowed for the establishment of American Indian schools. The first federally funded school for the Navajo people opened in Fort Defiance, Arizona, in 1869. The treaty provided for the construction of schools and for the hiring of one teacher for every twenty students. From the perspective of the American government, the American Indians needed to be civilized in the hope that peaceful relations between settlers and Indians could be achieved. Thus, education was accorded a primary role in this process. The treaty states:

> In order to insure the civilization of the Indians entering into this treaty, the necessity of education is admitted, especially of such of them as may be settled

> on said agricultural parts of this reservation, and they therefore pledge themselves to compel their children, male and female, between the ages of six and sixteen years, to attend school [57th Congress, cited in Terrell, 1970, p. 222].

Later, efforts were undertaken to proselytize among the Navajo people. In order to do this effectively, literacy instruction in Navajo for Navajo adults was begun on the Little Colorado River at the turn of the century. Fred Mitchell, a former YMCA worker from Topeka, Kansas, arrived at the Tolchaco Mission near Leupp, Arizona, in 1904. Mitchell had learned to speak Navajo and opened an Interpreter's Institute for Navajo Adults "to learn to preach the gospel in their own language and cultural context" (Dolaghan and Scates, 1971, p. 31). When Mitchell broke his back in a wagon accident, he spent his convalescence writing *Diné Bizaad: A Handbook for Beginners in the Study of the Navajo Language* (Mitchell, 1910). However, the work of teaching Navajo adults to read and write in Navajo ended in 1918 when the buildings at Tolchaco were destroyed by fire. Despite this setback, efforts to translate the Bible into Navajo continued among both Catholic and Protestant missionaries throughout the early years of the century.

In the 1930s, John Collier, Commissioner of Indian Affairs, provided government funds for Navajo language adult education in an effort to transform reservation schools into community institutions. Collier commissioned Yale linguist Edward Sapir to write a Navajo worker's handbook to introduce written Navajo to government employees. In the summer of 1934, as part of Collier's experiment in ethnic life, Gladys Reichard, a Barnard College linguist, held a summer hogan (a typical Navajo dwelling) school for teachers and interpreters near Ganado, Arizona. Reichard describes her students who met in a hogan with a blackboard, two low tables, a box, and three blocks of wood: "There were eighteen students ranging in age from twenty-two to perhaps fifty-five years. All could read and write in English. The students began to write compositions of their own about a week after starting" (Reichard, 1934, 24–20–1).

The following winter Collier appointed Father Berard Haile to conduct an Interpreter's Institute at Fort Wingate. Haile recorded the topics of literacy study: "We endeavored to record terminology in use at present for chapter organizations, their officials, the manner of voting, etc. A similar vocabulary was desired for community center work and day schools" (Haile, 1934). In 1934 Collier proposed the construction of twenty-five day schools that would provide community services for adults as well as education for children (Parman, 1976). He appointed Alan Hulsizer and Sally Lucas Jean, adult educators, and members of the Progressive Education Association to train Navajo administrators in community relations and tribal culture for the new schools.

These efforts to educate Navajo adults within their cultural context continued during World War II when Wycliffe Bible translators collaborated with U.S. Bureau of Indian Affairs employees to produce educational materials to teach adult literacy. Robert Young and William Morgan wrote articles and booklets on health, conservation, and livestock management (Lockard, 1993, 1995).

Young and Morgan published a bilingual dictionary in 1943 and a monthly Navajo language newsmagazine, *Adahooniligii*, which was distributed to six adult literacy centers on the Navajo Nation until 1957. In 1944, the tribal council distributed a pamphlet written in Navajo by Robert Young and William Morgan to encourage Navajo involvement in educational planning. Young writes, "Because of the cultural and linguistic barriers between Navajo society and non-Indian society, a primary problem in promoting Navajo participation in postwar educational planning is to develop understanding by Navajos of their needs and solutions for their betterment" (cited in Boyce, 1974, p. 141).

Following a postwar period of assimilation and an effort to relocate Navajo adolescents in off-reservation boarding schools, efforts to teach Navajo language to adults were renewed in the 1960s. The Rough Rock Demonstration School opened on July 27, 1966. The school was "regarded not just as a place for educating Indian children, but as the focus for development of the local community" (U.S. Congress, 1969). Rough Rock Demonstration School provided a model for contract schools that were locally controlled and that became centers for the development and dissemination of Navajo language curriculum materials (McCarty, 1989).

Rough Rock, Pine Hill, Rock Point, and Borrego Pass were the first locally controlled contract schools that recognized the need for teachers who were literate in Navajo and for basic literacy programs that served adults in the community. In the spring of 1992, more than twenty-five years after the founding of Rough Rock Community School, members of a teacher study group reflected that the school was not a place where they would have to listen to one person to give them all the answers. Dick, Estell, and McCarty point out that over this period of time Rough Rock "teachers strengthened their appreciation for their bilingualism and knowledge of the community as resources for teaching" (1994, p. 42). This sense of shared community is an underlying theme in successful adult Navajo language literacy programs. The roots of Navajo language instruction in adult education are traced to the efforts of missionaries, government agents, and teachers. In the following sections of the chapter, four successful adult education programs that trace their success to this tradition of cultural teaching will be discussed.

Programs to Restore the Past, Inform the Present, and Foresee the Future

In the past few years, several adult education programs that serve Navajo adults in their native language have achieved a noteworthy level of success. The adult literacy program at the Arizona State Prison, the Diné College teacher pre-service program, and the East Community School in Salt Lake City, Utah, each provide an example of culturally and linguistically grounded education programs for Navajo adult learners.

Arizona State Prison Navajo Literacy Program. The first program for Navajo language literacy in adult education focuses on inmates in the Arizona state prison system who work in small, informal study groups to learn to read and write in Navajo. The goal of this program is to restore cultural pride, which has been eroded by substance abuse and incarceration.

Alvin Tsingine, a Navajo inmate and former reservation adult educator, describes his students:

> At the present time there are many Navajo teenagers and others in their early 20s that are coming through here that have minimal Navajo language speaking ability or understanding of reading and writing it. . . . Upon release, we wish to return to our Sacred land and the People better prepared to listen to our Elders to live in the Beauty Way and Harmony of our culture and traditions [letter to the author, May 4, 1997].

He writes of the purpose for studying Navajo literacy:

> The majority of Native Americans on this yard are Navajos that have a limited English education. Being ordered to assimilate and being stripped of our cultural and traditional heritage leads Native Americans to violent intentions and rebellious attitude toward the Establishment. I believe that teaching with the use of first language is more productive and gives a more positive mood for learning and retaining knowledge. We have a beautiful language that must never die. I believe that teaching English through the use of students' first language brings about more comfortable communication and a more harmonious environment where the students become more willing to learn. My objective is to prepare those students for GED testing. . . . Instead of speaking of gangs, violence and causing trouble I'm trying to have these Navajo youth use their time more productively by learning to speak their Native language. Over 75 percent of these Navajos are currently enrolled and attending college computer classes so I know that they have the aptitude to learn and there is plenty of time for learning as they have little to do while sitting in their cells day after day [letter to the author, May 4, 1997].

Anthony Billings, a Navajo instructor, meets twice a week for thirty minutes to an hour with a group of students. He writes, "The class begins with a review of new sounds and new words that the students have learned or practiced. The words and sounds are practiced in simple sentences. The practice includes reading aloud and writing new words" (letter to the author, May 5, 1998).

Billings describes one successful student who has broadened his literacy study to include Navajo history. He writes, "This student loves to hear the Navajo tongue. He is patient and steady in his studies" (letter to the author, May 5, 1998). The instructor continues to describe the sociocultural foundation of the language and literacy study by stating, "Students become more bounded through the study of Navajo. As one learns the language one also becomes more closely related to the people whose language it is" (letter to the author, May 5, 1998). Navajo language instruction in prison settings empowers inmates to examine their history, to recover their voices, with the goal of rejoining the community of Navajo language speakers outside prison on their release.

Diné College Teacher Pre-Service Program. The second program for Navajo language literacy in adult education focuses on preserving and teaching the Navajo language to future generations. To accomplish this goal, the program trains teachers to integrate Navajo language and history into existing courses. Because many Navajo adults grow up without formal instruction in written Navajo, the practical consequence of this program is to encourage native language literacy among Navajo adults so they can learn about their cultural heritage.

Pre-service teachers enroll in eight semester-long courses in Navajo language and culture at Diné College—a tribal college with sites throughout the Navajo Nation. The students, who are employed as paraprofessionals in public schools and Bureau of Indian Affairs schools on the Navajo Nation, attend Navajo language classes after school and during summer sessions in their own communities. The majority of the students are fluent speakers of Navajo who participate in a variety of cultural events in their local communities. However, few of these adult students received instruction in Navajo literacy during their own K–12 education. Today these pre-service teachers are studying Navajo to teach in bilingual-bicultural classrooms and to preserve their language and culture for future generations. The experiences of two individuals—Helen Dineyazhe, a pre-service teacher and her Navajo language instructor, Martha Jackson—underscore the success of the program.

Helen Dineyazhe, a 1997 graduate of Northern Arizona University, works as a Title VII Curriculum Specialist at Chinle Primary School. She works with bilingual classroom teachers to prepare Navajo language thematic units that focus on culturally relevant content area instruction. She discusses how she studied Navajo literacy at Diné College and how learning to read and write in Navajo prepared her for her teaching career.

Dineyazhe, daughter of a bilingual first-grade teacher at Chinle Primary School, spoke English as a child. When she entered the Navajo Teacher Education Project she enrolled in Navajo 101 and 102: Navajo for Non-Native Speakers. Her instructors encouraged her to think in Navajo, and she began to practice grammatical substitution drills while jogging. Dineyazhe read children's books in Navajo and asked colleagues and family members questions about the language. As Dineyazhe gained proficiency in oral and written Navajo, she enrolled in Navajo 211 and 212: Navajo for Native Speakers. Her proficiency in reading helped her to become a better speaker. Her instructors, O. J. Becenti and Martha Jackson, both of whom are Navajo, encouraged her to use her interest in music in preparing class presentations. Dineyazhe wrote songs in Navajo that she published and taught to the class. For an oral history project, Dineyazhe interviewed elders in the community in Navajo about their early schooling experiences. The elders told her that they had been hit with a wooden spoon as punishment for speaking Navajo in their dormitory rooms. Dineyazhe uses these stories to improve her ability to record and transcribe oral Navajo. Her records serve as a reminder of changing attitudes toward Navajo language and as an example of the importance of respecting her students.

Dineyazhe's instructor, Martha Jackson, uses sketches and photographs from the community to allow students to explore their language and their culture. In one lesson the instructor observed students discussing a photograph of a winter hogan and recorded students' comments in Navajo on the chalkboard. Jackson (1991) writes,

> It looks lonely with a heavy cloud in the back. No sheep or any livestock or no woods and no footprints. The clouds were very mean looking, some were white and others gray masses of white and others gray masses of water and ice above the hogan. It's dark, threatens, obscures, seems to be moving. The snow looks deep and cold [p. 40].

Jackson's students generated a vocabulary list in Navajo and English, and the class read the list from the chalkboard. Students dictated sentences using these vocabulary words, and the instructor used these key sentences to write a group story on the chalkboard. The story was typed and reproduced for students to read aloud in small groups.

Students use this growing body of student writing to increase fluency (Slate, Jackson, and Goldtooth, 1989). They also read the *Rock Point Community School Newspaper,* as well as readers produced in the 1970s by the Native American Materials Development Center, and the *Navajo Times,* a biweekly Navajo language newspaper.

Jackson's students write a variety of texts in Navajo such as notes for oral presentations, class notes, lists, personal journals, and rough drafts. Students also write in Navajo for class assignments. In such writing they record Navajo jokes, oral histories transcribed for class presentations, radio scripts, essays on cultural issues, video scripts, and writing integrated with content area coursework. Peers who are fluent, native speakers of Navajo edit these assignments. These exercises in Navajo language literacy help adults continue to use the Navajo language at home. Many Diné college students are speaking Navajo at home with their children for part of the day and inviting relatives to participate in Navajo language activities in their homes to help teach the language to their children.

Helen Dineyazhe enrolled in Navajo language literacy classes at Diné College and used community resources to gain proficiency in her ancestral language. Today, she uses examples from her study of Navajo language and culture to inform her own teaching practice. Dineyazhe shared her success as a language learner during a panel discussion with dual language educators at the Eighth Annual Bilingual Education Institute at Arizona State University in November 1998. As a Navajo language teacher she uses her language to transform the educational setting.

East Community School in Salt Lake City. The third program for Navajo language literacy in adult education focuses on building a community of adults who are literate in Navajo in an urban setting. The purpose of this adult education program is to foster a greater sense of community and cohesion among Navajo adults. At East Community School in Salt Lake City, Utah, where courses in Navajo, Lakota, and Ute language have been offered for the past twelve years, students use a variety of materials to study Navajo, including textbooks, audiotapes, and bilingual children's picture books. Students recognize the unique strength and resilience of their Navajo language and culture in an urban setting. Navajo language classes are scheduled for three, eight-week sessions a year in Salt Lake City school buildings.

Instructors in the Navajo language program are native speakers who work with Native American adults in community service institutions. One instructor is a social worker; the other is a teacher and school guidance counselor. The students are Navajo men and women who range in age from the early twenties to the late sixties and come from a variety of socioeconomic backgrounds and occupations—from health care professionals to welfare recipients. As is often the case, only one or two students in each class have a productive knowledge of Navajo. Students read children's picture books in Navajo and use audiotapes from the textbook series *Diné Bizaad: Speak, Read, Write Navajo* (Goossen, 1994) to introduce Navajo language literacy in a communicative setting. Throughout the course, students pose many questions about Navajo culture and history, which are integrated into the study of the language. Marilyn Williams, the program coordinator, recognizes the students' need for cultural identity in an urban setting as the central purpose for enrolling in the Navajo language literacy class. This sense of cultural identity is integrated in the curriculum and pedagogy of the East Community School program through the use of native instructors and through the teaching of Navajo culture throughout the curriculum.

The Family and Child Education Program: Linking Generations

The Family and Child Education (FACE) Program at the Bureau of Indian Affairs School in Teec Nos Pos, Arizona, links the teaching of Navajo language literacy between generations. Children ages three to five attend an early childhood education program while a parent is enrolled in an adult education program. Parents and children engage in daily literacy activities during parent and child (PAC) time for one hour each day.

During the first nine weeks of participation in the Teec Nos Pos FACE program, parents study the Navajo writing system. In the second nine weeks, they write and illustrate books for their children in Navajo. The technology component of the project allows parents to add these Navajo language books to their electronic literacy portfolios and share these culturally relevant curriculum materials with their children during PAC time at school and at home in the evening.

Navajo culture is an important component of the family literacy program. Community members teach a topic in Navajo culture for one hour a day during parenting time. A local silversmith leads parents in a month-long project. During the project, parents discuss a plan for a bracelet or necklace, design the project, measure and obtain materials, and complete the project. With the silversmith they discuss marketing strategies and sell their bracelet or necklace. Navajo elders come into the classroom to teach the history of weaving and to set up looms. The elders help parents begin the weaving process.

From time to time, a medicine man visits the class to discuss family values and the importance of traditional teaching in Navajo. This instruction in Navajo culture is conducted in a hogan. By holding class in a traditional Navajo structure, as well as teaching Navajo cultural traditions and Navajo language, parents gain a stronger sense of cultural identity. As a consequence, they transmit a sense of appreciation for Navajo cultural heritage to their children and also renew the connections between traditional cultural knowledge and literacy.

Al Begay, the FACE adult educator, says in an interview with the author that the program works well because Navajo culture views things as a whole (interview with the author, August 1998). When parents study Navajo language literacy to share this skill with their children—when they bridge generations—they feel successful. Three parents who entered the program as welfare recipients have completed their GEDs and are currently enrolled in college.

Past, Future, Present

This chapter serves to establish the historical roots of community-based Navajo language literacy instruction. It also describes how Navajo literacy instruction for adults today is used to restore the past, build a community in the present, and prepare teachers and students for the future. These three goals may be achieved by teachers and students in any subordinate culture through the study of their ancestral language. Jim Cummins (1991) warns, "Valorization of minority students' language and culture directly addresses the ambivalence about their identity that students and communities often feel as a result of current and historical patterns of discrimination" (p. 5). Navajo language literacy in adult education programs will succeed when teachers and students recognize the counter-hegemonic force of native language literacy and when they act to reclaim their voice, history, and future.

Implications for Adult Educators

Adult educators can adapt instruction to Native American students if they recognize their students' ambivalence about cultural identity based on discrimination. This ambivalence, which is often manifested in the language shift from Navajo to English, must be addressed by adopting a curriculum that includes the native language and culture of the learners and that includes the study of cultural identity. Ambrose Yazzie, a secondary school educator, describes this link between loss of identity and loss of language when he says, "Throughout my education, I spoke Navajo. English was my second language. Today when I speak Navajo with my students they often respond in English. I tell them they should not be ashamed of speaking the Navajo language, that it is good to know two languages."

Adult educators can attempt to reverse the tide of language shift and cultural alienation that has limited human potential on the Navajo Nation and complicated efforts to solve social problems such as poverty, violence, unemployment, and school failure. The reversal of language shift requires the training of teachers who are bilingual. Justin Jones, director of the Navajo Division of Education, writes,

> We concur with the need for more competent bilingual teachers in the classroom to better teach our Navajo children and to develop instructional materials that are relevant to the culture of the Navajo people. . . . professionals are scarce and much in demand . . . the Navajo Nation has been engaged in supporting and training Navajo teachers for the past few years, but due to its limited resources has not been able to serve many more paraprofessionals and other students who have interest in becoming teachers on the Navajo Nation [personal communication, January 1998].

The Diné Division of Education has begun systemic reform and is seeking to implement the Diné language and culture teaching perspective. This cultural perspective incorporates the Diné philosophy of learning, which has four components: (1) respect for nature, (2) standards (positive attributes) for life, (3) social competence, and (4) making a living. Navajo adult educational programs, therefore, are based on the following premises: (1) education is best when it reflects a sense of place; (2) education should be based on the philosophy and values of those being educated; and (3) the preparation of teachers and mentors should reflect the Diné perspective of education.

At each site where this reform is being implemented there is a reciprocal relationship between the schools and the community involving the community in the identification of themes and issues to be explored in the teaching process and involving students in field research. In each site, a series of relational learning opportunities has been developed in which the values of place and culture are reinforced.

The Navajo Tribal Education Policy (1984) proposes bilingual education for all schools. The policy states:

> The Navajo language is an essential element of the life, culture, and identity of the Navajo people. The Navajo Nation recognizes the importance of preserving and perpetuating that language for the survival of the Nation. Instruction in the Navajo language shall be made available for all grade levels in all schools serving the Navajo Nation [p. 3].

As culturally based Navajo literacy instruction is made available in schools, community centers, prisons, and tribal colleges, speakers of Navajo can regain their cultural heritage and the sovereignty of their language.

References

Boyce, G. *When Navajos Had Too Many Sheep: The 1940s*. San Francisco: Indian Historical Press, 1974.

Cummins, J. "Preventing Pedagogically-Induced Learning Difficulties Among Indigenous Students." *Journal of Navajo Education*, 1991, *8* (3), 3–9.

Dick, G., Estell, D., and McCarty, T. "Saad naakih Bee'enootiilji Na'alkaa: Restructuring the Teaching of Language and Literacy in a Navajo Community School." *Journal of American Indian Education*, 1994, *3*, 1–46.

Division of Diné Education. *Rural Challenge Project: Learn in Beauty*. Flagstaff, Ariz.: Division of Diné Education, 1997.

Dolaghan, T., and Scates, D. *The Navajos Are Coming to Jesus*. South Pasadena, Calif.: William Carey Library, 1978.

Giroux, H. "Literacy and the Pedagogy of Political Empowerment." In P. Freire and D. Macedo (eds.), *Introduction to Literacy: Reading the Word and the World*. South Hadley, Mass.: Bergin & Garvey, 1987.

Goossen, I. *Diné Bizaad: Speak, Read, Write Navajo*. Flagstaff, Ariz.: Salina Bookshelf, 1994.

Haile, B. *Papers*. University of Arizona Library, Tucson, 1934.

Jackson, M. "Joshua Led Me to the Classroom: Ha'at'ii Ei Iiyiisii baa Akoniizii' Doo Bohool'aa' La?" *Journal of Navajo Education*, 1991, *8* (2), 31–41.

Lockard, L. "Navajo Literacy: Stories of Learning to Write." Unpublished doctoral dissertation, College of Education, University of Arizona, 1993.

Lockard, L. "New Paper Words: Historical Images of Navajo Language Literacy." *American Indian Quarterly*, 1995, *19*, 17–29.

McCarty, T. "School as Community: The Rough Rock Demonstration." *Harvard Educational Review*, 1989, *59*, 484–503.

Mitchell, F. *Dineh Bizaad: A Handbook for Beginners in the Study of the Navajo Language*. Tolchaco, Ariz.: Mission to the Navajo Indian, 1910.

Navajo Tribe. *Navajo Nation Education Policies*. Window Rock, Ariz.: Navajo Division of Education, 1984.

Parman, D. *The Navajos and the New Deal*. New Haven, Conn.: Yale University Press, 1976.

Reichard, G. "Gladys Reichard Papers." Museum of Northern Arizona, Flagstaff, 1934.

Slate, C., Jackson, M., and Goldtooth, T. "Navajo Literacy in a Postsecondary Setting: Work in Progress at Navajo Community College." *Journal of Navajo Education*, 1989, *8* (1), 10–12.

Terrell, J. *The Navajos*. New York: Harper & Row, 1970.

U.S. Congress. "Indian Education: A National Tragedy—A National Challenge." 91st Congress, 1st session 1969, Report 91-501.

LOUISE LOCKARD is visiting assistant professor of education at Northern Arizona University.

6

African American adult education has long been centered in the antiracist struggle. A new dialogue is needed in order to rekindle the desire to end racism by finding creative educational approaches to old problems.

Creating a Culturally Relevant Dialogue for African American Adult Educators

Elizabeth A. Peterson

Since the Civil War brought an end to slavery in the United States, education for African Americans has been rooted in the antiracist struggle (hooks, 1994) and is therefore a political as well as social activity. Historically, teachers in the African American community were respected leaders; their knowledge gave them entry into the white man's domain of economic security, privilege, and power.

Currently, education for African Americans in general does little to connect African American people with their history of struggle. Today, a great deal of literature focuses on the need for teachers to emphasize cultural diversity in the classroom. Multicultural education has become a fad with teachers. They make certain that they mention famous minorities in their history lessons, adding International Day or Black History Day to the yearly calendar and carefully selecting textbooks in which "people of color" are represented. Over the years these minor changes to the curriculum have done little to help African Americans further the struggle for racial justice. Nor have they sufficiently dealt with a continuing problem: the denial of the basic rights and opportunities to individuals based on skin color. Education for African Americans needs to strengthen its focus on the antiracist struggle with new strategies for surviving in a racist society.

The History of African American Adult Education

Early in the struggle, a rift occurred between leaders whose different worldviews set them apart—in opposition to each other—regarding the educational needs of African Americans (Potts, 1996). Booker T. Washington and W.E.B. Du Bois elevated the debate over African American education to a national level when these two respected leaders openly clashed over their beliefs about the needs of former slaves and a strategy for integrating African Americans into American society (Potts, 1996). Washington took the more pragmatic approach and advocated a slow pace and hard work for black citizens that would not threaten the white power holders. Du Bois' more radical position "emphasized the need for African Americans to be self sufficient and to earn a decent living" (Potts, p. 34) and that the opportunity for all but the most menial work was often denied African American people. Du Bois recognized that all of the ills faced by African Americans could be linked to the "continued ignorance and lack of opportunity for many in the black community" (p. 34).

Other African American leaders and educators planned and implemented successful programs that met the needs of the African American men and women who eagerly came to learn (Peterson and Fisher, 1996). Individuals who were fortunate enough to participate in these programs had the opportunity to learn "useful knowledge" that would enable them to prosper economically and at the same time focus on their unique experiences as African Americans.

Fannie Jackson Coppin founded the Institute for Colored Youth in Philadelphia, where she successfully combined a classical liberal arts education and vocational training (Peterson, 1996b). Marcus Garvey centered the development of the Universal Negro Improvement Association (UNIA) in the African American struggle (Colin, 1996). He recognized the devastating effect of institutional racism on the African American community and developed educational programs "for African Ameripeans [sic], by African Ameripeans, with the socio-educational goal of education for selfethnic reliance" (p. 47).

The Harlem Renaissance: An Era of Growth. While Garvey was advocating for the complete separation of African Americans from the influences of the white-controlled educational agenda, the American Association of Adult Education (AAAE) was founded. This is significant because the Carnegie Corporation was influential in the creation of the AAAE. Carnegie's agenda in adult education extended the arm of white philanthropy into the African American community. Carnegie, under the auspices of the AAAE, commissioned two "experiments" in the African American community to determine if any one form of adult education (liberal, vocational, or cultural) would be more effective for African Americans (Guy, 1996). Harlem and Atlanta were selected as sites for this research, and in each case the programs developed were based on the needs of the local community. In Harlem "a broad based program that had cultural and civic content was conceived. What resulted was a conception of adult education that attempted to provide education for the masses of people by emphasizing matters of racial interest" (Guy, p. 94). The Atlanta project also developed out of the needs of community, but rather than focus on generic community needs, the program was designed to satisfy the many constituencies in the community. There were groups for women and other groups for public school teachers. The teachers discussed a variety of issues from international concerns to educational issues. Perhaps most important, the Atlanta project had an adult literacy component. A partnership was reached with the Atlanta University Education Department in an attempt to assist those adults who could not read.

Alain Locke, the first African American Rhodes Scholar, was chosen to evaluate the two projects. His remarks clearly support the need for adult education in the African American community. He suggested that the Harlem and Atlanta experiments be replicated in "every considerable Negro community in the country" (cited in Guy, 1996, p. 97). However, despite the apparent success of both programs and Locke's favorable review, both programs were terminated at the end of 1934. Guy (1996) writes that the termination of the Atlanta and Harlem projects is not surprising. The Carnegie Corporation's and the AAAE's interest in African American adult education was experimental. Perhaps, the understanding of the transient nature of white support was what inspired Marcus Garvey and his supporters to advocate that African Americans seek control over their own destiny by financing, developing, and governing programs that meet their needs.

During the first half of this century, initiatives in the African American community continued to develop, flourish briefly, and then quietly die away. In time, Marcus Garvey was deported and the support of the Carnegie Corporation and AAAE for African American adult education waned. The next big push for African American adult education came during the civil rights movement.

The Civil Rights Movement: The Great Push for Social Justice. The significant role that adult education played in the overall framework of the civil rights movement deserves special mention in any history of African American adult education. Unlike the Civil War (which many whites refer to as a war fought primarily for states' rights, with slavery as a secondary concern), the focus of the civil rights movement was the end of legalized discrimination in the United States. Civil rights activists were encouraged to believe that racism would be wiped out when discrimination was outlawed. It was assumed that the end of legal discrimination would open up new opportunities for African Americans and therefore allow for the complete integration of African American people into mainstream American society. Most often the history of the civil rights movement is focused on the actions of one man, Martin Luther King Jr., who fervently believed in the power of nonviolent resistance. King (1956) writes:

> We can act in the struggle in such a way that they will see the error of their approach and will come to respect us. Then we can all live together in peace and equality. . . . We do not wish to triumph over the white community. That would only result in transferring those now on the bottom to the top. But, if

> we can live up to nonviolence in thought and deed, there will emerge an interracial society based on freedom for all [cited in Washington, 1986, pp. 80–81].

King recognized that education was an essential element of nonviolent "struggle" and in 1961 asked Septima Clark to become the director of education for the Southern Christian Leadership Conference (SCLC). Four years earlier Clark had formed the first Citizenship School on John's Island, South Carolina (Easter, 1996). The purpose of the program was "not only to teach them how to read and write but to teach them at the same time things they would have to know in order to start on their way to becoming first-class citizens" (Clark, cited in Easter, p. 118). Clark expanded this approach as head of education programs for the SCLC and developed a course that "gave poorly educated rural African Americans a crash course in the American political system" (Clark, cited in Easter, p. 119). Later, King would refer to the success of American Jews and write that true "Black Power" would emerge by "uniting social action with educational competence" (King, cited in Washington, 1986, p. 311).

King was not the only African American leader to emerge during this time period. While King was encouraging the African American community to engage in nonviolent resistance, others thought that African Americans had been nonviolent for too long. Malcolm X and the Nation of Islam blasted the notion that nonviolent protest would someday lead to an integrated, interracial society. Malcolm X believed that the racial hatred of African Americans would always prohibit racial integration. He goes on to say that integration in and of itself is not even important to most African Americans. "Human rights! Rights as *human beings!* That's what America's African American masses want. . . . The American black man should be focusing his every effort toward building his *own* businesses, and decent homes for himself" (Haley, 1964, p. 272). The Nation of Islam created educational programs that were significantly reminiscent of Marcus Garvey's UNIA. These programs shifted the focus of education away from racial integration to one of social and economic independence. Malcolm X states:

> The word "integration" was invented by a Northern liberal. The word has no real meaning. I ask you: in the racial sense which it's used so much today, whatever "integration" is supposed to mean, can it precisely be defined? The truth is that "integration" is an *image*, it's a foxy Northern liberal's smokescreen that confuses the true wants of the American Black man [p. 272].

By the time Malcolm X was assassinated in February 1965, he had amended many of his previous beliefs and saw the possibility that African Americans and well-meaning whites could work together in the struggle for human rights. After his rift with the Nation of Islam he founded a new organization, the Organization of Afro-American Unity, as a "non-religious, non-sectarian, group organized to unite Afro-Americans for a constructive program toward attainment of human rights" (Haley, p. 416).

Cries for racial unity were repeated by many other groups and individuals active in the civil rights and African American liberation movements of the 1960s and 1970s. Another group that deserves mention for its work to bring about change in the African American community is the Black Panther Party. The Black Panthers, founded in 1966 by Bobby Seale and Huey Newton, grew out of the violence that erupted in northern urban centers. From the beginning this group had a more radical message. The leaders stressed the need for African American people to unite, control their own destiny, and protect themselves—even if this meant bearing arms. The Panthers organized a number of initiatives such as free medical clinics and breakfast programs that were much needed in the inner cities. The Panthers' outspoken political agenda called for educational programs framed in the context of struggle. Teachers and students specifically addressed the nature of the political process and devised strategies to combat injustices committed in the African American community.

Culturally Relevant Adult Education: A Continuing Need in a Changing World

The unrest of the 1960s subsided as legislation was enacted to put an end to legal racial discrimination. On the surface the climate of the 1970s was more liberal; many individuals involved in the struggle stepped back, certain that the strife of the 1960s had passed and that African Americans would prosper and flourish. African American educators watched as the civil rights battle for school desegregation was being won, and it seemed that the "dream" of equal opportunity might be realized.

Ladson-Billings (1998) writes:

> This notion of equal opportunity was associated with the idea that students of color should have access to the same school opportunities, that is, curriculum, instruction, funding, facilities, as White students. This emphasis on "sameness" was important because it helped boost the arguments for "equal treatment under the law" that were important for moving African Americans from their second class status [p. 18].

Integration had not proven to be the solution for the racial ills of this nation. The dream was for African Americans to have the benefit of the same (and it was assumed better) education as whites. Unfortunately, this also meant that African American students, who had previously been taught and nurtured by African American faculty who understood their needs, were now often taught by white teachers who had not developed a sensitivity for their new students. They often judged differences in appearance, speech, and mannerisms as inferior to the white students with whom they were more familiar. To explain this phenomenon of racial preference, Derrick Bell (1992) offers the concept of "racial nepotism," and he asserts that due to racial nepotism, racism will always exist.

> But nepotism, I objected, is a preference for family members or relatives. What does it have to do with racial discrimination?. . . . Then it hit me. . . . You're suggesting that whites tend to treat one another like family, at least when there's a choice between them and us. So that terms like 'merit' and 'best qualified' are infinitely manipulable [sic] if and when whites must explain why they reject blacks to hire 'relatives' —even when the only relationship is that of race [p. 56].

Bell goes on to suggest that as long as people exercise the right to align, first with those who are family and then with those who make up an extended family based on race, no legislation can be enforced that will totally eliminate discriminative practice. He proposes that a new dialogue on race is needed—one that moves away from the belief that racism can be eradicated through legislation and enforcement to a dialogue that acknowledges that racism will always exist and that we must find ways to either work around it or use it to our benefit. He contends that racist behavior ends only when it is no longer beneficial to those who exhibit it. This theory has now been given the name *critical race theory* (CRT) and has promise as a means of creating a richer dialogue regarding culturally relevant adult education.

Defining Critical Race Theory

Ladson-Billings (1998) offers a definition of CRT. She states that "CRT is a link between form and substance in scholarship which allows scholars the 'use of voice' or 'naming your reality' through parables, chronicles, stories, counterstories, poetry, fiction and revisionist histories to illustrate the false necessity and irony of much of current civil rights doctrine" (p. 12).

CRT grew out of the work of Derrick Bell, who recognized that "traditional legal approaches to civil rights (filing briefs, conducting protests, marches, and appealing to the moral sensibilities of decent 'citizens' produced smaller and fewer gains than in previous times" (p. 10). CRT scholars sometimes use storytelling to "analyze the myths, presuppositions, and received wisdoms that make up the common culture about race and that invariably render blacks and other minorities one down" (Delgado, cited in Ladson-Billings, p. 11). CRT allows theorists to draw on their experiential knowledge of race and racial matters.

CRT is a critique of liberalism that contends that the push for civil rights is necessarily a long, slow, and uphill struggle. "Critical race" theorists believe that racism will be eliminated only when sweeping changes take place (Bell, 1992, p. 12). Bell, among others, has criticized traditional civil rights policies because they are based on the idea that racism can be solved through the legislative and judicial processes, giving rise to social policies such as affirmative action. As long as the African American leadership remains so focused on legal procedures, creative strategies that would help

African Americans live and thrive in a society that may never resolve issues of racism are not even considered.

Bell (1992) illustrates this point in a story, "The Racial Preference Licensing Act." In this story, the Racial Preference Licensing Act is an option for all white employers, proprietors of public facilities, and owners and managers of any housing facilities who wish to engage in discriminatory practices. Those wishing to exercise this option would be required to purchase a racial preference license for a sizeable fee. Once obtained, the government requires payment to a government commission of a tax of 3 percent of the income derived from the whites employed, served, or products sold to whites during each quarter in which a policy of racial preference is in effect. Any nonlicensed employer that practices discrimination is to be fined. The money collected in fees and fines goes into an "equality fund" to directly benefit the African American community—loans for small businesses and scholarships. In this manner the African American community is benefited rather than harmed by white racism. CRT theorists argue that whites have been the primary beneficiaries of civil rights legislation and "new radical approaches are needed to surmount the nation's continuing tensions over racial status" (p. 52).

Connections to Adult Education

CRT supports the need for an expanded dialogue on the role of education in the African American community. Through this process it might be possible to design creative new programs that meet the needs of African Americans at numerous stages of growth and development. One thing is clear: whites have benefited throughout history from treating all African Americans as if they are exactly the same, with little regard for regional, socioeconomic, and gender differences that might contribute to the way individual African American people experience the world. The they're-all-alike misconception has resulted in one-size-fits-all solutions that have in some cases worked for some African American people, opening doors and providing opportunities, but have failed miserably in eliminating the social, economic, and political disparities between the races. In adult education one-size-fits-all approaches to literacy can be used as an example of how this approach has failed. Currently, most literacy programs have employed "deficit approaches" that emphasize the poverty, the lack of skills, and failures of the students enrolled. In some cases these students have very low skills but this is not always true. By always focusing on students' lack of skills and failure to learn, other problems that have an impact on adult literacy are ignored (for example, adult learning disabilities, the poor quality of some schools, and academic tracking).

The failure of integration to lift African Americans from their second-class status is another example of how one-size-fits-all thinking has failed. Using CRT we can better understand how "experiences of race" can have an impact on program directors, teachers, and learners. We can evaluate the success of traditional educational programming by examining four essential aspects of program planning and design: curriculum, instruction, assessment, and funding.

Curriculum. School curriculum is often biased. According to Ladson-Billings (1998) the official school curriculum is a "culturally specific artifact designed to maintain a White supremacist master script" (p. 18). The master script deletes or distorts the stories of African Americans, especially those who challenge the power and authority of the dominant culture. Traditional approaches to "opening up" the curriculum (including the contributions of African Americans and other minorities) have not been effective in most cases. More often than not, information about select minority leaders is inserted into the existing curriculum as if they were honorable mentions in a curriculum otherwise dominated by whites. Currently, there is a call for a colorblind perspective that celebrates the diversity of this nation, maintaining that "we" are all immigrants. Ladson-Billings warns that this "misequating the middle passage with Ellis Island" injures African American, Native American, and Chicano students who feel guilty, wondering why they have not been able to rise above immigrant status as others have (p. 18).

Racial bias often prevents African Americans from receiving access to an enriched curriculum, even within a seemingly integrated system. Ability tracking (based on purported "scientific" measures of ability) has been one way that students have been resegregated. African American students are more often placed in remedial courses that do not adequately prepare them to compete with whites either in academic settings or in the workplace. Tracking has been billed as a noble attempt to help support African American students; in reality, white students have benefited from a tracking system that segregates them in "regular" or sometimes even "enriched" courses that are academically challenging.

Instruction. Ladson-Billings (1998) suggests that current instructional strategies presume that African American students are deficient. "As a consequence, classroom teachers are engaged in a neverending quest for 'the right strategy or technique' to deal with (read: control) 'at risk' (read: African American) students" (p. 19). The "at risk" label follows the African American student throughout a lifetime of educational encounters. It is even applied to African American students who otherwise possess no other "at risk" characteristics (poverty, single-parent families, a history of abuse or neglect) except race.

Assessment. There have been many attempts to prove that African Americans are inferior to whites based on intelligence tests. African Americans are often at a loss on intelligence tests that measure the quality of schooling as much as they measure innate intelligence. "In the classroom, a dysfunctional curriculum coupled with a lack of instructional innovation (or persistence) adds up to poor performance on traditional assessment measures" (Ladson-Billings, p. 20).

Funding. Critical race theorists contend that inequalities in program funding are a function of institutional and structural racism. Therefore, it is no coincidence that adult basic education (ABE), which is perceived as a program that enrolls a larger proportion of African American students than other public and private adult education programs, is so often underfunded. In a survey of adult education programs in South Carolina, Peterson and Fisher (1996) found that ABE programs on average received $250 a year per student. During the same year the wealthiest school districts received as much as $2,500 per student. Many adult literacy programs rely upon volunteer support and operate without the support of full-time paid staff. In one South Carolina county the ratio of students to staff (paid and volunteer) was 33 to 1 (Peterson, 1996a).

The disparity in funding current educational programs is perceived by many to be fair. Money is spent where it is most needed (on children). Adult education is funded at a much-reduced rate with federal and state funds that are allotted on a per student basis. The exception would be workplace programs, where employers invest a great deal of money for basic skills instruction that is integrated into a job-related curriculum. I heard a program director say that he agreed that adult basic education and literacy programs should not be considered a priority: "I agree with most folks who feel that they paid for these people to go to school and get an education the first time around. If they didn't get it, then I don't feel that the taxpayers should pay the second time around for their (adult students) failure." As long as individuals in decision-making positions label the students as failures (thinking failure is due to students' refusal or inability to learn what they, as decision makers, have decided they should learn), few changes will be made.

A New Dialogue for Adult Educators

In March 1998, Lani Guinier, law professor and critical race theorist, in a speech at the University of South Carolina, used the analogy of the "miners' canary" to describe the new dialogue that is needed to combat racial injustice in the United States. She explained how coal miners always went into the mines with a canary. Any changes in the canary's condition served to warn the miners that the air in the mine was becoming toxic. The miners then would come out of the mine before they were harmed. She asserted that African Americans have been America's canary. When the African American community is in turmoil, the unrest ultimately spills over and has a serious impact on white America; the "air becomes toxic" for all. Civil rights legislation, enacted to open up doors for African Americans and other minorities, opened up doors for poor whites, who were also finding it difficult to access and benefit from social structures designed for the rich.

Guinier was making the point that rather than throw out programs like affirmative action, the entire structure should be analyzed to determine who really benefits from the system and who does not; then leaders can work to develop creative new systems that work better for all people. This approach could prove very helpful for educators as well. Creating culturally relevant programs in adult education is more than an issue of inclusion. Including references to famous African Americans and acknowledging African American customs and traditions in the curriculum can do little to expel racism. What is needed is a more thorough examination of racism in adult education. What we might discover is that the civil rights battles that we fought in the past for educational reforms so desperately needed have benefited many people of all colors. But some side effects were never anticipated.

For example, the ill will created by the upward mobility of middle-class African Americans is one of the civil rights side effects. Bell (1992) provides a story that illustrates how reform has backfired on the African American community, creating a climate of distrust: Bell is in a cab, rushing to a speaking engagement and deeply involved in a conversation with the cab driver, Jesse B. Semple. Semple is a down-to-earth man who, if circumstances had been different, could have been an academic. He is able to hold his own with the noted law professor. Semple explains how the advances of the African American middle class have hurt poor African American people:

> I mean no offense, but the fact is you movin'-on-up black folks hurt us everyday blacks simply by being successful. The white folks see you doing your thing, making money in the high five figures, latching on to all kinds of fancy titles, some of which even have a little authority behind the name, and generally moving on up. They conclude right off that discrimination is over, and that if the rest of us got up off our dead asses, dropped the welfare tit, stopped having illegitimate babies, and found jobs, we would all be just like you [p. 26].

This point of view is important for all educators, but especially African American educators, to understand. The distrust that this statement implies illuminates a real issue in the African American community—the growing rift between classes. Whites often refer to the problems of the African American community as a problem that "they" should solve for themselves by practicing the model of "racial nepotism" that other groups have employed. Yet, as hooks (1995) writes:

> They [privileged African Americans] see themselves as more deserving. Unlike underclass and underprivileged African American people, they have a sense of entitlement. And it is the sense that they will be selected out and treated better, bred into them at birth by their class values, that erupts into rage when white folks arbitrarily choose to make no distinction between a black person from an "elite" class and someone from the underclass [p. 28].

The issue of distrust that arises from differences in class is critical. We must begin a dialogue about culturally relevant adult education by addressing the issues of class that keep us apart. We cannot practice "racial nepotism" when African Americans who have "made it" resent and blame their underclass "brothers" because they feel that they are responsible for any mistreatment that they might receive. There can be no "uplift" when the underclass resents their more affluent and better-educated "sisters" because they feel they have turned their backs on them, at the same time leaving them vulnerable in an abusive society.

I first became aware of this when I was a teacher in an ABE classroom. One young woman was very resistant and did not seem to respect me as her teacher. One day in class she blurted out that what I was teaching her was not at all useful. She had real problems: she was in an abusive relationship, her children needed school clothes, she had no money, and everyone she went to for a job turned her away. She was faced with the possibility that she would have to go to her boyfriend for money and that he would give it to her but then use that as an excuse to beat her. Her question to me was, "How can you tell me anything? You with your good education and nice job; you've never had to struggle in your life? What can you tell me about someone having their boot in your back?" Her anguish opened up an opportunity for true dialogue. I was able to explain to her that, yes, on the surface it appeared that life had been kinder to me but that I too understood struggle, that I had been denied opportunities and faced rejection. I shared some of my story; my willingness to do so gave others courage to share theirs as well. Trust developed out of that one incident, and we were then able to learn from one another. Lessons that before had seemed irrelevant had value. They trusted me when I told them that what they were learning could be useful. We used this one woman's dilemma to problem solve. How could we help her? How could we help ourselves? In this case we were able to mediate our class differences by focusing on a struggle that we all understood.

Today, there are many "hot topics" in education. For example, the use of Ebonics in the classroom is a topic that requires a constructive dialogue in the African American community. Many well-educated African Americans have denounced the notion that Ebonics (which they regard as bad English) should ever be taught in school. They reject the notion that a language that is used in many urban centers throughout the nation should receive English-as-a-second-language status and funding support for instruction. Other educators regard the use of Ebonics in the classroom as a strategy that can help teachers bridge the gap between the students and themselves. Smith (1998) found that the young adults she taught in an alternative high school were much more open and receptive when material reflected their reality and they were allowed to use their own language. She quotes one student as saying, "You have no right to make us stop saying these words. It's the way we talk. It offends me for you [the teacher] to treat me like I wouldn't have sense enough to know when I should not use them" (p. 82).

CRT might allow African Americans with opposing viewpoints to speak from their own experiences about the power of language within this society.

Important questions such as these could be addressed through this kind of critical dialogue: Why is standard English regarded as the language of power?, What assumptions do adult educators make about people who use other forms of English?, or Is the use of Ebonics ever appropriate?

Ebonics is just one topic that requires the attention of African American educators. Africentric educational models, special projects for African American males, and academic and social tracking are all issues that could be more effectively addressed through a constructive dialogue that allowed individuals to share their stories.

Conclusion

Historically, African American adult education has been rooted in the antiracist struggle. We cannot afford to lose sight of this common thread that unites us all, regardless of class. According to hooks (1995), we need to "engage in race talk" and invite everyone to share their stories regardless of race, gender, or class. We have all struggled in an environment that has too often been toxic. It is unfortunate that early leaders like Booker T. Washington and W.E.B. Du Bois never realized that they were more alike than different. They were united in the antiracist struggle.

The civil rights movement was the one time in history when the African American community was so committed and unified around a common cause. Adult education was central to the movement, and it was so powerful because the antiracist struggle was at the heart of all activity. Adults learned to read for the first time in order to read ballots and voting regulations. They learned to write in order to sign their names at the polls. Middle-class African Americans were joined in solidarity, helping their less fortunate neighbors because they realized how important they were to the cause. Everyone sensed the urgency of the moment. Whites joined the movement and worked side by side with people they had never before worked with as equals. A white friend recently told me that in her opinion, "whites who became involved in the civil rights movement learned just as much as African Americans; there was so much going on at that time that was brand new."

Whites and nonwhites cannot share an experience of "race," so differences must be mediated through education. Education becomes relevant when it creates an opportunity for us to better understand and appreciate one another. The antiracist struggle continues.

References

Bell, D. *Faces at the Bottom of the Well: The Permanence of Racism.* New York: Basic Books, 1992.

Colin, S.A.J., III. "Marcus Garvey: Africentric Adult Education for Selfethnic Reliance." In E. Peterson (ed.), *Freedom Road: Adult Education of African Americans.* Malabar, Fla.: Krieger, 1996.

Easter, O. "Septima Poinsette Clark: Unsung Heroine of the Civil Rights Movement." In E. Peterson (ed.), *Freedom Road: Adult Education of African Americans*. Malabar, Fla.: Krieger, 1996.

Guinier, L. (untitled speech). University of South Carolina Law School. Columbia, S.C., 1998.

Guy, T. "The American Association of Adult Education and the Experiments in African American Adult Education." In E. Peterson (ed.), *Freedom Road: Adult Education of African Americans*. Malabar, Fla.: Krieger, 1996.

Haley, A. *The Autobiography of Malcolm X*. New York: Ballantine Books, 1964.

hooks, b. *Teaching to Transgress: Education as the Practice of Freedom*. New York: Routledge, 1994.

hooks, b. *Killing Rage: Ending Racism*. New York: Henry Holt, 1995.

King, M. L., Jr. "Black Power Defined." In J. Washington (ed.), *A Testament of Hope: The Essential Writings and Speeches of Martin Luther King, Jr.* San Francisco: Harper & Row, 1986a.

King, M. L., Jr. "Our Struggle." In J. Washington (ed.), *A Testament of Hope: The Essential Writings and Speeches of Martin Luther King, Jr.* San Francisco: Harper & Row, 1986b.

Ladson-Billings, G. "Just What Is Critical Race Theory and What's It Doing in a Nice Field Like Education?" *International Journal of Qualitative Studies in Education*, 1998, *11* (7), Jan.-Mar., 7–23.

Peterson, E. "Breaking the Bonds of Literacy in South Carolina: A Challenge for the Black Community." In K. Campbell (ed.), *The State of Black South Carolina*. Columbia, S.C.: The Columbia Urban League, 1996a.

Peterson, E. "Fannie Coppin, Mary Shadd Cary, and Charlotte Grimke: Three African American Women Who Made a Difference." In E. Peterson (ed.), *Freedom Road: Adult Education of African Americans*. Malabar, Fla.: Krieger, 1996b.

Peterson, E., and Fisher, S. *The Midlands Literacy Checkup*. Columbia, S.C.: The United Way of the Midlands, 1996.

Potts, E. "The Du Bois-Washington Debate: Conflicting Strategies." In E. Peterson (ed.), *Freedom Road: Adult Education of African Americans*. Malabar, Fla.: Krieger, 1996.

Smith, E. "The Impact of the Bibliotherapeutic Experience: Reaching the At Risk Student." Unpublished doctoral dissertation, College of Education, University of South Carolina, 1998.

Washington, J. *Alain Locke and Philosophy: A Quest for Cultural Pluralism*. Westport, Conn.: Greenwood Press, 1986.

ELIZABETH A. PETERSON is associate professor of adult education at the University of South Carolina, Columbia.

7

Key themes and purposes of culturally relevant adult education are discussed.

Culturally Relevant Adult Education: Key Themes and Common Purposes

Talmadge C. Guy

Some years ago noted sociologist William Julius Wilson (1987) wrote a book titled *The Truly Disadvantaged.* His thesis was that economic inequality had grown to the point that a permanent underclass of Americans had been created. This underclass, according to Wilson, cut across racial and ethnic lines, was primarily urban, undereducated, and unemployed—in fact, was unemployable. Although Wilson's argument was based mainly on an analysis that minimized the significance of culture, ethnicity, or race—points with which I disagree—he did make an important point relevant to the discussion here: inequality is endemic to the American system and, unless something specific occurs to prevent it, it will remain so. This pessimism about the ability of the American social system to foster its own cure for radical inequality and oppression is echoed by other scholars. Derrick Bell (1992), noted legal scholar, argues that America is inevitably racist and that little can be done to change the status of African Americans as a marginalized minority in America.

From a historical perspective, it cannot escape even the most casual observer that many of the same ethnic, racial, and linguistic groups who suffered the greatest oppression in the United States at the dawn of the twentieth century continue to suffer great oppression at the dawn of the twenty-first century. African Americans, Hispanic Americans, Native Americans—to name some obvious examples—continue to struggle for opportunity and equity. This is true despite drastic changes to American society. The discussions presented by the contributors to this volume attest to the continuing problem of continuing social inequality. No matter how much conservative educators or politicians desire to wish it away, social injustice afflicts racial, ethnic, linguistic, and culturally marginalized groups in the United States. Educational strategies, models, and practices that do not explicitly challenge the status quo only serve to reproduce it.

The chapter authors have discussed the important issue of marginalized group culture as it affects the lives of learners in adult education classes; some authors have described educational strategies that assert or reclaim what Amstutz identifies as alternative types of knowledge. It is precisely this "fugitive knowledge" that Freire (1997) refers to in *Teachers as Cultural Workers*. To paraphrase Freire: when men and women realize that they themselves are the makers of culture, they have accomplished, or nearly accomplished the first step toward feeling the importance, the necessity, and the possibility of their own freedom. It is this goal that is central to the notion of culturally relevant adult education as discussed in these pages.

In culturally relevant programs, adult educators strive to help learners who face oppression on a daily basis take control of their lives. Adult education, on these terms, aids in turning learners' lives around so that they become strong, confident, agents of change not only for themselves but for their families, their communities, and the country. By examining the possibilities of cultural education—education that focuses on the positive aspects of learner culture and uses that knowledge to help learners recreate a world in the image of their own dreams—adult education strives to achieve within cultural communities the goal of social equality.

Although the authors in this volume approach the topic of culturally relevant education from different educational roles and contexts, they hold a number of themes in common. In the following section I discuss some of the most important ones, with an eye to further defining and clarifying the aims, purposes, and processes of culturally relevant adult education.

Theoretical Issues in Learning

In her chapter, Amstutz lays out how adult education learning theory has progressed to greater degrees of refinement in ways that reflect the educational and learning experiences of groups previously excluded from educational discourse. The idea of a generic adult learner with certain universal characteristics and traits is rejected by all of the authors. In each case, the particular sociocultural context in which learners exist and act strongly influences the motivations, needs, goals, and perspectives that learners bring to the learning environment. As Amstutz argues, understanding these aspects of adult learners and their implications for adult learning is significant if adult education is to become culturally relevant. Sheared and Lockard present the case for adult educators to acknowledge and incorporate aspects of the adult learners' culture into the educational process.

From a policy standpoint, Jeria and Peterson raise important issues regarding the particular social circumstances of African Americans and Hispanic Americans as adult learners and the implications of these for educational policy and programming. The research on which they base their discussions, however, needs to be amplified and extended. We simply do not know enough about the variety of cultural issues that particular cultural groups bring to the educational environment. As Amstutz points out, "The congruence between learner communication style and learning preferences based on learner cultural background is crucial." Even though a good deal of research has been conducted on learner cultural background in K–12 educational settings, much remains to be done in the field of adult education. However, the research cited by the chapter authors begins to provide a clear image of the adult learner as conditioned by the sociocultural environment in ways that affect participation, the quality of the learning experience, and the educational outcomes.

Learner Transformation. Another theme shared among the authors is that of learner transformation. Overcoming adverse political, social, cultural, linguistic, economic, or educational conditions is explicitly addressed by each author. The means by which this can be accomplished is directly related to how learners view themselves and their ability to change their environment. Learner self-image—seeing oneself in a positive light and being supported in that self-perception by other learners and educational officials (teacher, administrators, and so on)—is therefore a crucial aspect of culturally relevant adult education.

Related to this notion of learner identity is the concept of community. In each of the foregoing chapters, the discussion of learners is always in relation to a particular community that holds significance and relevance for the learner. Whether that community is bounded by language, culture, geography, or history, the learner sees himself or herself as a member of a community that shares important attributes. Lockard states this concisely when she says, "[Navajo] language learning is central to the development of cultural identity which, in turn, is an important aspect of being Navajo in the modern world." Adult educators who work with marginalized groups of learners need not underestimate the power of community and its impact on the educational experience of the learner.

Empowerment. The striving for empowerment is a central aspect of culturally relevant education. *Empowerment* has many meanings, but in the context of this discussion it certainly has to do with both individual and social transformation. Furthermore, it is suggested that learners who retain internalized negative or passive images of themselves are marginalized by the dominant culture. The dominant culture operates in such a way as to diminish the ability of marginalized learners to challenge the circumstances of their marginalization. Therefore, to challenge the authority and power of the dominant culture is central to culturally relevant adult education. In discussing critical race theory (CRT) as a frame for adult education, Peterson argues, "Critical Race Theory might allow African Americans with opposing viewpoints to speak from their own experiences about the power of language within this society." The point is that the value of CRT, or any educational perspective or model, is relative to its ability to help learners challenge the status quo that oppresses them.

An essential point in this discussion is that the power to change is already present in the learner. It is not given or handed over by the adult educator or any other authority figure. Latent power is characteristic of all learners. In the case of racially, ethnically, or linguistically marginalized learners, the goal of culturally relevant adult education is to realize the latent power within the learner by helping the learner to "see" the power capability within.

Community-Based Programming and Public Policy. The use of culturally relevant strategies in adult education has significant implications for how and where culturally relevant adult education programs are housed and run. Sheared notes that the traditional funding support for ABE programs adversely affects literacy workers' ability to create innovative programming. Similarly, Peterson notes that "inequalities in program funding are a function of institutional and structural racism." Resource and financial constraints, coupled with negative views toward race-based or ethnic-based programming, limit the possibility of culturally relevant programming within formal educational institutions.

The alternative to this is to organize community-based programs and services so that the decision-making and control mechanisms will serve the needs of the target population. Of course, the difficulty with this strategy is that it potentially exacerbates the resource problem, leaving many effective programs without a sufficient resource base and incapable of expanding services. Nevertheless, a clear theme emerges that adult educators should be creative in finding resources and gaining institutional or community support for programs.

The Politics of Cultural Difference. The integrated nature of history, public policy, and learner sociocultural environment points to the political nature of education. Power disparities between dominant and marginalized cultures are reflected in the oppressed condition of learners from marginalized cultures. Dominant culture retains the institutional authority to enforce its view of what is right, good, normal, useful, or best. The mere celebration of learner culture is insufficient to address the serious problems associated with learner-lived experiences for the culturally marginalized learner. Learners need to understand the political context of the relationship between their home or native culture and that of the mainstream. They also need to understand how their cultural identity is potentially oppositional to mainstream norms, values, and practices.

For example, Jeria cites how American Nativism affects the negative view of Hispanics and ignores the historical realities in which Hispanics' experience in America "is the experience of colonialism and discrimination." This historical reality has contributed to the rise of contemporary prejudices against Hispanics who are often viewed as illegal aliens on the very land that Spanish-speaking peoples occupied prior to the arrival of Anglo-Americans, especially in parts of the South and Southwest. Consequently, to assert the right of Hispanics to bilingual adult education programs is to affront the cultural and political sensibilities of the mainstream.

Difficult Issues

Despite the favorable reports in this volume, there remain some difficult issues for practitioners who engage in culturally relevant adult education. I summarize these briefly in the sections to follow.

Adult Educator Cultural Awareness. Most professional preparation in adult education ignores the issue of culture as a significant factor in adult education programs and services (Amstutz, 1994). Consequently, adult education practitioners who serve racial, ethnic, or linguistically marginalized learners often are forced to either reexamine their assumptions about learners or impose their prejudices and biases on learners. This is reflected in the language used to refer to learners who are often viewed from a deficit perspective: lazy, incapable, unintelligent, unmotivated, and so on. These assumptions serve to disempower learners and to reproduce educational and social inequality. And they do not recognize the power within learners to take control of their circumstances. Adult educators must examine the assumptions they hold about learners, about learning, and about the educational process. It is impossible to adequately conceptualize or effectively work with learners from other cultural backgrounds without first challenging one's own assumptions, beliefs, and values about who the learners are.

Identity, Community, and Democracy. The goal of education is ultimately to change individuals and the community. For this to occur, individuals need to see themselves as part of a larger community. Separatist or exclusionary perspectives, therefore, do not aid in the achievement of individual and social change. Adult educators should avoid encouraging the development of ethnocentric or chauvinistic attitudes among learners. Valorizing one's own sociocultural perspective at the expense of others is to reverse the dominant-subordinate cultural relationship and subvert meaningful change. Adults from marginalized communities need to see themselves as viable members of a democratic society. They need to see themselves as contributing not only to the welfare of their own communities but also to the larger society. Antonia Darder (1991) refers to the state of being in two cultures at the same time as biculturalism—the condition that marginalized adults must achieve if they are to create change within their community and the larger society.

Adult Educator as Political Agent. The role of the adult education practitioner takes on significantly political overtones. This does not mean that educators must run for political office. It does mean, however, that without an adequate political analysis of the sociocultural condition in which learners exist or the political insight and skill to advocate for learners' needs and rights, the adult education practitioner has a limited ability to adequately represent the issues and needs of learners or of the program in which he or she works. Curriculum policy, funding, program organization, and staffing, as well as relationships with other agencies that serve the target population, require that the adult educator be clear about program goals and objectives.

A case in point is the firestorm of controversy that developed following the announcement in 1996 by the Oakland school board that an Ebonics program for teachers would be employed to help African American students learn English. Despite educational and linguistic research demonstrating the viability of the program, the Oakland Plan, as it came to be known, was widely attacked and condemned. Without the political strength and acumen to defend this program, the Oakland school board's proposal would surely have fallen by the wayside. Similar proposals for culturally relevant language instruction in adult literacy programs have been met with objection and controversy. In such cases adult educators need to be prepared to take on the opposition and to articulate and clarify why such programs are needed.

Conclusion

Unless adult educators develop educational strategies that respond directly to the sociocultural environment in which marginalized adult learners find themselves, it is unlikely that significant progress will be made toward addressing the problems of inequality and social injustice in marginalized communities. It is urgent that adult educators explore creative and culturally relevant approaches to serving marginalized adult learner populations, because the numbers of adults in these communities is projected to grow through the middle of the next century. By beginning where learners are and with what they know best—their own cultural background and setting—adult educators can help learners take charge of their lives and have an impact on their communities—and the wider society.

References

Amstutz, D. "Staff Development: Addressing Issues of Race and Gender." In E. Hayes and S. A. Colin III (eds.), New Directions for Adult and Continuing Education, no. 61. San Francisco: Jossey-Bass, 1994.

Bell, D. A. *Faces at the Bottom of the Well: The Permanence of Racism*. New York: Basic Books, 1992.

Darder, A. *Culture and Power in the Classroom: A Critical Foundation for Bicultural Education*. New York: Bergin & Garvey, 1991.

Freire, P. *Teachers as Cultural Workers: Letters to Those Who Dare to Teach*. Boulder, Co.: Westview Press, 1998.

Wilson, W. J. *The Truly Disadvantaged: The Inner City, the Underclass, and Public Policy*. Chicago: University of Chicago Press, 1987.

TALMADGE C. GUY is assistant professor in the Department of Adult Education at the University of Georgia, Athens.

INDEX

Other Titles Available in the New Directions for Adult and Continuing Education Series
Susan Imel, Editor-in-Chief

ACE81 Enhancing Creativity in Adult and Continuing Education: Innovative Approaches, Methods, and Ideas, *Paul Jay Edelson, Patricia L. Malone*
ACE80 Women's Career Development Across the Lifespan: Insights and Strategies for Women, Organizations, and Adult Educators, *Laura L. Bierema*
ACE79 The Power and Potential of Collaborative Learning Partnerships, *Iris M. Saltiel, Angela Sgroi, Ralph G. Brockett*
ACE78 Adult Learning and the Internet, *Brad Cahoon*
ACE77 Using Learning to Meet the Challenges of Older Adulthood, *James C. Fisher, Mary Alice Wolf*
ACE76 New Perspectives on Designing and Implementing Effective Workshops, *Jean Anderson Fleming*
ACE75 Assessing Adult Learning in Diverse Settings: Current Issues and Approaches, *Amy D. Rose, Meredyth A. Leahy*
ACE74 Transformative Learning in Action: Insights from Practice, *Patricia Cranton*
ACE73 Creating Practical Knowledge Through Action Research: Posing Problems, Solving Problems, and Improving Daily Practice, *B. Allan Quigley, Gary W. Kuhne*
ACE72 Workplace Learning: Debating Five Critical Questions of Theory and Practice, *Robert W. Rowden*
ACE71 Learning in Groups: Exploring Fundamental Principles, New Uses, and Emerging Opportunities, *Susan Imel*
ACE70 A Community-Based Approach to Literacy Programs: Taking Learners' Lives into Account, *Peggy A. Sissel*
ACE69 What Really Matters in Adult Education Program Planning: Lessons in Negotiating Power and Interests, *Ronald M. Cervero, Arthur L. Wilson*
ACE68 Workplace Learning, *W. Franklin Spikes*
ACE67 Facilitating Distance Education, *Mark H. Rossman, Maxine E. Rossman*
ACE66 Mentoring: New Strategies and Challenges, *Michael W. Galbraith, Norman H. Cohen*
ACE65 Learning Environments for Women's Adult Development: Bridges Toward Change, *Kathleen Taylor, Catherine Marienau*
ACE62 Experiential Learning: A New Approach, *Lewis Jackson, Rosemary S. Caffarella*
ACE60 Current Perspectives on Administration of Adult Education Programs, *Patricia Mulcrone*
ACE59 Applying Cognitive Learning Theory to Adult Learning, *Daniele D. Flannery*
ACE57 An Update on Adult Learning Theory, *Sharan B. Merriam*
ACE54 Confronting Controversies in Challenging Times: A Call for Action, *Michael W. Galbraith, Burton R. Sisco*
ACE49 Mistakes Made and Lessons Learned: Overcoming Obstacles to Successful Program Planning, *Thomas J. Sork*
ACE45 Applying Adult Development Strategies, *Mark H. Rossman, Maxine E. Rossman*
ACE44 Fulfilling the Promise of Adult and Continuing Education, *B. Allan Quigley*
ACE43 Effective Teaching Styles, *Elisabeth Hayes*

Back Issue/Subscription Order Form

Copy or detach and send to:

Jossey-Bass Inc., Publishers, 350 Sansome Street, San Francisco CA 94104-1342

Call or fax toll free!

Phone 888-378-2537 6AM-5PM PST; Fax 800-605-2665

Back issues: Please send me the following issues at $23 each.
(Important: please include series initials and issue number, such as ACE78.)

1. ACE ________________________________

____

____

$ __________ Total for single issues

$ __________ Shipping charges (for single issues ***only;*** subscriptions are exempt from shipping charges): Up to $30, add $5⁵⁰ • $30⁰¹–$50, add $6⁵⁰ $50⁰¹–$75, add $7⁵⁰ • $75⁰¹–$100, add $9 • $100⁰¹–$150, add $10 Over $150, call for shipping charge.

Subscriptions Please ❑ start ❑ renew my subscription to *New Directions for Adult and Continuing Education* for the year____ at the following rate:

❑ Individual $58 ❑ Institutional $104

NOTE: Subscriptions are quarterly, and are for the calendar year only. Subscriptions begin with the spring issue of the year indicated above. For shipping outside the U.S., please add $25.

$ __________ Total single issues and subscriptions (CA, IN, NJ, NY and DC residents, add sales tax for single issues. NY and DC residents must include shipping charges when calculating sales tax. NY and Canadian residents only, add sales tax for subscriptions.)

❑ Payment enclosed (U.S. check or money order only)

❑ VISA, MC, AmEx, Discover Card # ____________________ Exp. date ________

Signature ____________________ Day phone ____________

❑ Bill me (U.S. institutional orders only. Purchase order required.)

Purchase order # ____________________

Name ____________________

Address ____________________

____

____

Phone ____________________ E-mail ____________________

For more information about Jossey-Bass Publishers, visit our Web site at: www.josseybass.com

PRIORITY CODE = ND1